LIONS

THE GERMAN LIST

Hans Blumenberg

# LIONS

TRANSLATED BY KÁRI DRISCOLL

LONDON NEW YORK CALCUTTA

This publication was supported by a grant
from the Goethe-Institut India

**Seagull Books, 2018**

First published in German as *Löwen* by Hans Blumenberg
© Suhrkamp Verlag, Frankfurt am Main, 2001
All rights reserved by and controlled through
Suhrkamp Verlag, Berlin.

First published in English by Seagull Books, 2018
English Translation and Notes © Kári Driscoll, 2018

ISBN    978 0 8574 2 430 3

**British Library Cataloguing-in-Publication Data**
A catalogue record for this book is available from the
British Library

Typeset by Seagull Books, Calcutta, India
Printed and bound by Hyam Enterprises, Calcutta, India

CONTENTS

# LIONS

If lions could paint, their hunters would be the hunted.

La Fontaine tells of a painter who exhibits a painting of a fearsome lion that has been brought down by a solitary hunter. The viewers seem to appreciate the painting above all because the hunter, as a representative of their species, has demonstrated man's superiority over the king of the beasts. Evidently, however, they have been a little too loud in congratulating themselves. A lion has overheard them and attributes their vaunted superiority entirely to the painter's imagination. In just two lines he sets things straight: *Avec plus de raison nous aurions le dessus, / Si mes confrères savoient peindre.*

Aesthetically, the lion's intervention has the advantage of not presenting a more realistic counter-example. Despite having appeared on the scene *in natura* and not merely *in figura* in order to criticize the painter and his audience's arrogance, he limits himself to ascribing the same degree of imagination and success to his conspecifics. The only difference being that painting is not part of a lion's repertoire.

Just as well, as anyone who owns an edition of La Fontaine's fables with the illustrations by Grandville will appreciate. The latter's etching for this particular fable shows a lion standing on his hind legs, holding a brush and palette in his front paws, putting the finishing touches to a lurid scene in which a lion, far more terrifying than the artist, towers over a vanquished human victim of pitiful proportions. There are no prizes for the worst possible illustration, but if there were, this would surely take first place.

The lion in the fable is precisely *not* asking the enthusiastic gallerygoers to imagine a lion painting but, rather, wishes above all to save his species from the ignominy of mere aesthetics. In his kingly politeness, he tactfully avoids giving the arrogant admirers of this painter's flattering depiction any bloody counter-examples, in order to show them that the pleasure they derive from the painting rests precisely on its avoidance of reality. Instead it is enough for him to demonstrate the relativity of each species' self-confidence at the aesthetic level of comparison: it ought to be possible by purely rhetorical means to persuade these people, who want only to imagine how one of their own kind might vanquish a lion, to imagine how lions would handle an equivalent situation—if only they possessed the power of aesthetic imagination. But it is imperative that we hold on to the premise that lions do not in fact paint. Which is why they have to be predators instead.

Meanwhile, let us observe what a magnificent accomplishment of the rational mind is the subjunctive. It would permit even a lion to become a protector of men.

## SYMPATHY FOR THE LION

It is curious, writes Alfred Polgar in one of his essays, to see which sorts of people prefer which sorts of animals. Young Lotte, a delicate little girl, was fond of lions, those broad-nosed bandits. A life-long preference, as it turned out.

Somewhat uncharacteristically, Polgar failed to take this observation to its logical conclusion. And yet he was but a single step away from the ultimate degree of generality: how curious it is that people should prefer animals at all.

Indeed, dainty little Lotte would have provided him with the finest motivation for this last step, for she played the starring role in an anecdote about a little girl who bursts into bitter tears at the sight of a painting entitled *The Persecution of Christians under Nero*. When asked the reason for her distress, she points to a solitary lion cowering glumly in the corner of the painting and poignantly exclaims, 'Oh, Daddy, that poor lion hasn't got a Christian!'

How outrageous such injustice can be if only the distribution of goods is seen from the appropriate distance; such as the distance between this compassionate child and the lions and their abstract right to Christian fare. All lions—how could it be otherwise?—are created equal, and if Christians are what is for dinner, then naturally there must be enough for everyone.

In 1855, Friedrich Hebbel notes down in his diary a curious snippet by the medieval encyclopedist Vincent of Beauvais, the author of the *Speculum maius*, which he claims to have taken from an Arabic source, and which the *Weimarische Jahrbuch* had seen fit to reproduce for its readers in its inaugural issue in 1854: *The lion becomes feverish at the sight of a man. To cure himself of the fever, he must devour an ape. Similia similibus.*

What might have inspired Hebbel to copy down this cryptic fable?

Hebbel returned again and again to the metaphor of cannibalism. In it, he hoped to find the solution to the problem posed by his impotence as a playwright: that of creating people. The only way to do that seems to be that of ancient magic, namely, by eating them. Emil Kuh—his long-time friend, and later apostate until their deathbed reconciliation, who atoned for his apostasy by slaving away at Hebbel's biography, dying of consumption before he could complete it—gave the most terrifying summation of his idol's existence: *Undoubtedly, Hebbel was a man-eater, a brain-predator, and what drew some of us to him, to the point of limitless devotion, was not only love and enthusiasm but also that terrible natural force that renders the bird powerless in the face of the snake, or that pulls the vertigo-stricken into the abyss.* Hebbel had practically spoken these exact words to Kuh himself. When asked about renting an apartment in the countryside outside Vienna, he replied, 'What for? I have no need of such things; I need the big city! I devour people!'

Hebbel enjoyed his reputation in Vienna as a fearsome outsider, a man capable of anything; lying in wait for his prey so he could finally put a piece of life on stage at the Burgtheater, which refused for so long to stage his plays. Van Bruyck reports running into him on the street: *He looked like a man who might commit a murder at the next moment.* Eduard Hanslick attributed Hebbel's lack of interest in the visual arts and, especially, in music to his indifference to nature and its beauty. He tells the same story as Kuh, though with a slight variation. In his version, an acquaintance had wanted to congratulate Hebbel, who had recently purchased a country house in Gmunden, on his new property in such beautiful surroundings, to which Hebbel replies: 'Spare me that endless talk of the pleasures of nature. I don't eat cockchafers, I eat people.'

Cannibalism might be described as the absolute metaphor of his self-conception: the hidden confession of his tragic impotence. Eating people, if these witnesses are to be believed, is Hebbel's most naive and candid expression of what he feels that people owe him, so that he in turn can bring people into being.

And then he comes across this medieval story about the lion's homeopathic self-medication. The lion satisfies his feverish hunger for man, his only rival in the animal kingdom, by consuming the latter's distorted image, his caricature: the ape. Hebbel does not comment on such discoveries. Indeed, he probably did not fully understand what it was about this vignette that had caught his attention. Did it hint at a solution to his problem? And if so, what was it?

An absolute metaphor: by definition, it cannot be reduced to a formula.

## THE ELEPHANT, NOT THE LION

Schopenhauer was disappointed with the lion for failing to live up to the requirements of his metaphysics of the Will and its relation to sexual desire, but this deficiency was made up for by the elephant, which helped to lend impressive shape to a different aspect of his philosophy. Schopenhauer acknowledged this with one brief postulate: *The Idea of the elephant is imperishable*. If the resilience of childhood impressions from the zoo and the circus are any indication, one is inclined to agree with Schopenhauer's statement.

But why the idea of the elephant, specifically? The extent to which this animal's appearance on the European horizon impacted the public's intuition and imagination cannot be explained in purely psychological terms. If, for Schopenhauer, that which he calls the 'Idea' is not derived from the intuitive perception of transcendental objects but, rather, from their empirical existence through a form of concentration—a revision of Kant's 'disinterested delight' —then the elephant might induce something like the shortest transition from empirical to pure intuition. This would be due not to the exotic strangeness of its form but to the lack of differentiation in its prodigious, space-filling mass.

Its 'essence' is therefore quickly, nay, instantaneously graspable; and this in turn demonstrates the proximity of the Real to the Ideal. And yet, while form and mass exert an optically palpable resistance to any attempt at domination—a resistance that persists even though the patient labour of domesticated animals would seem to confirm our ability to dominate them—such intractable resistance can be linked to the ease with which our intuition may idealize such forms. Thus, the disinterestedness of our intuition is supported, much like when we gaze at the starry heavens.

What creates such a strong impression is the raw power required for mere existence, the sense of the connection between matter and Will, between the mass and its visibility. This power seems so aware of its inviolability that the physical appearance of this animal cannot carry a trace of artifice, of mimicry, or of dissimulation.

Schopenhauer's notion of the 'power to exist' distils that which, in opposition to need, and by means of dissemblance, cunning and the instrumentalization of visibility, allows man to remain in existence. This metaphorical power has to do with the distinction, which Schopenhauer borrowed from Kant and further refined to use against him, between appearance and the 'thing-in-itself'. The 'thing-in-itself', to which neither extension nor duration can be attributed, 'imparts' the 'power to exist' to everything that has extension and duration—i.e. which exists in space and time according to relations of causality. Hence the 'thing-in-itself' is not primarily a factor in sensory affection but, rather, the 'power' that expresses itself in the unity of the predicate of existence of things and which gives them their permanence and resistance. The term suggests that the existence of phenomena is not self-evidently a form of inertness in the absence of external influence. Instead—we see it in the elephant—existence must be 'pushed through' [*durchgesetzt*] despite the diffuse, amorphous resistance of matter.

The metaphor of power—or, more precisely, of the relation between mass and power—is the instrument Schopenhauer uses to slip the Will behind the scenes of nature, behind all her appearances, all the forms of things. Thus, the old Aristotelian link between matter and form and their 'existence' would be reconstituted, albeit with an inverted constitutive relation. Matter, thanks to this hidden power with which it is endowed, is now causality itself; not merely one of the four causalities. And yet its quality has remained unchanged. As a substrate of power, it aids the Will's demonic ground of being in realizing its own principle: the insufficient reason for everything.

The Idea, however, finding expression in the powerful form of mass and offering itself to intuition, is at once the inadvertent end product of the Will and also by that very fact the only possibility of resisting it and its life-oriented power. That power must be rendered intuitively evident if one is to avoid blindly submitting to it. And so the elephant becomes the ally of the philosopher, because it seems to have achieved sufficient distance from the basic principle of human existence, that of unrelenting self-preservation. Or, indeed, it brings it into view.

## THE ABSENCE ABOUT THE LION

In 1867, having fled Russia to escape his creditors, Dostoevsky and his new wife Anna Grigoryevna decided to stay in Dresden, the better to be able to return. After all, their involuntary exile was only supposed to be temporary: surely his luck at the roulette table would soon turn and all their problems would be solved. Fedya has already been out a couple of days to try his luck and is unfazed by the loss of his gambling money.

Anna Grigoryevna kept a diary, which is an extraordinary document of this period. She was a stenographer, and so her entries are marvellously detailed. At this point, she does not yet seem to be entirely sure what to make of her new husband, and their eternal quarrels and evening reconciliations seem like tests of strength for the future separation of their roles in the marriage. Her husband is still an unknown quantity to her, and she is exploring the room to breathe that he gives her. The strictly provisional nature of their situation, in which everything must be subordinated to the swift satisfaction of the creditors, while all the while the boredom of this ever-expanding period of time begins to weigh upon them, lends an air of irreality to everything the great realist and his young bride do.

And so, one day, for the price of five silver groschen per person, they visit the zoological gardens, where they observe three beavers and a white peacock, and finally, in the pungent smell of the wild animal house, a tiger and a leopard, as well as four lions, all pacing restlessly back and forth in their narrow cages. In front of the cage where a big, mature lion is being kept separate from the lioness, Fedya, confident as ever in his strength and his luck, puts the power of his gaze to the test (or is that merely the impression he wanted to give Anna?). As she recalls it that evening in her diary, Fedya looks at that lion *so hard* that the lion begins to run around his cage with increasing agitation and rage, and then to roar, softly at first and then more and more loudly, till he is answered by the lioness in the adjacent cage: *They roared so dreadfully I began to fear lest the railings should give way and they would come bursting out of their cages, which would have been no laughing matter. Never in my life have I heard such a terrific roaring.*

So this was another thing her Fedya could do: hit his mark as surely as at the shooting gallery. But at the same time, the wise old lion had also shown him what it is like when one is separated from one's lioness and only the penetrating gaze of a stranger can rekindle the desire for a conjugal roar. This scene makes Anna marvel at something she does not yet understand: vicariously, she has witnessed a power that she will come to experience first-hand. The most fundamental source of her amazement, however, is the fact that Fedya can dominate this lion so completely, even though the latter's receptivity to the charm of this stranger's gaze is diminished by half: the lion has only one eye.

# FIESCO'S LION

*Tell me not of that lion, but go home and think upon him.*
Thus Fiesco, Count of Lavagna, concludes his demagogical speech to the people of Genoa, who, according to Schiller's stage directions, have stormed into his palace, *breaking down the door*, and, following the rhetorical transformation of their 'indignation' [*Empörung*] into 'conspiracy' [*Verschwörung*], *depart tumultuously*, taking with them his enjoinder to think upon the lion.

The lion is the centrepiece of Fiesco's classicistic parable. The political history of Genoa up to its liberation from the French by Andrea Doria and his odious nepotism is presented as an animal fable. Once upon a time, a bulldog exploited the unrest in the animal kingdom in order to seize the throne, whereupon, in accordance with his canine nature, he *gnawed on his subjects' bones*. This led to revolt, regicide, parliament, democracy. But this form of government proved inadequate when humans declared war on the *newly minted republic*. The horse and the lion, the elephant and the rhinoceros sounded the call to arms, but from the lamb and the hare and the birds and the fishes came the whimpering and fearful call for peace—and they were in the majority. And so the animal kingdom was subdued and *man plundered its territory*.

Another system of government was called for. Fiesco shrewdly asks the Genoese for advice and they suggest a democracy of councils. Now the wolves are the financiers, the doves preside over the criminal courts, the tigers and goats over the civil courts, the asses are the ambassadors, the mole is inspector-general of the administration, the hares are the soldiers, while the lions and the elephants are in charge of the baggage. Of course, each animal abuses its office in accordance with the traits of its species; but in the end, it is the mole who declares everything to be in order. Another era ends in revolution. This time a monarchy is established: the new ruler should have claws and a brain and, above all, just *one* stomach. Therein lies the economic principle of this solution. All hail the lion.

The demagogue need not draw the conclusion, the people have understood: And *Genoa also shall follow that example. Genoa already has its man.* No one in the audience at the 1784 premiere in Mannheim will have been surprised at this outcome.

And yet this rhetorical fable is unusual in one respect: the lion is crowned king of all the animals, which means he has to *become* king; he hasn't always *been* the king for ever and ever, be it by virtue of his strength or his grace. The political history of the animal kingdom moves from one crisis to the next and the reasoning that finally leads to the investiture of the lion has nothing to do with pompous appeals to the magnificence of his configuration as a creature, nor with any justification of his kingly nature as evinced by the entire fable tradition. To be sure, he is one of the strongest, but not *the* strongest of all the animals mentioned. He has both claws and a brain—which makes up for the failures of the previous regimes. But the real justification for allowing the lion, endowed with these advantages, to ascend to the royal throne, delivered at the high point of the argument, is that he has but *one* stomach and that his other attributes guarantee that there will be need for but *one* of his kind—regardless of how excessive his appetite may be. Whether he can be of any use is irrelevant; after the tumultuous events in the animal kingdom's history it is the assurance that he will not be an undue burden on the people that constitutes his entire populist appeal.

The lion has become a figure of late historical consciousness, stripped of his genuine attributes and transformed into heraldic figuration. He is the master of the moment of perplexity. He is lacking too much to be the object of original, archaic enthusiasm and admiration, but at least there is only one of him, and he is the kind of animal who can accept there being only one.

## IMPEDED LIONS

For Henri 'le Douanier' Rousseau, the task of painting lions was a commitment unto itself. The only teacher besides nature he would name was Jean-Léon Gérôme, a successful academic painter whose speciality was representing the king of the jungle in every imaginable attitude of wildness fit for the Salon. At least two of the lions Rousseau painted are notable because of the contrast between them: on the one hand, the lion in *The Sleeping Gypsy* (1897), and, on the other, the hungry lion in the eponymous painting (1905).

The most obvious difference between the two paintings, namely, that the earlier one is set in the desert, the later one in the jungle, is immaterial with respect to Rousseau's lions. In the period between them, Rousseau had translated the greenhouses at the Jardin des Plantes into props for his works and had no more need of the austerity of the desert with this new abundance of sumptuous foliage at his disposal.

The Gypsy—if that is indeed what she is, and not rather a Mooress—is lying decoratively on the desert floor in the light of the full moon, beside her a mandolin and a water jug. In a well-draped, striped dress, she sleeps calmly and serenely, despite the fact that there is a lion standing over her, sniffing at her. The viewer is unlikely to feel any impending danger; rather, the interpreters of this image have generally presumed that the viewer will take the lion to have been dreamt up—not by the painter but, rather, by the sleeping woman. To be sure, dream-lions are allowed to appear as gentle as anything and still be lions. In any case, this possibly oneiric lion is certainly not based on a stuffed original, as Gérôme's was. It is more likely to have been a stuffed toy with glass button eyes, an artfully groomed tail and a crimped woollen mane. But the sleeper too lies there as if she were a mannequin the painter has borrowed for the occasion. Her posture is so stiff, it seems she has been made for that dress, not the other way around.

But we can ignore all of that once we begin to ask what it is that the painting lacks in order for it to live up to Rousseau's ambition of being a 'Realist' painter. The answer might be that Realism has an olfactory dimension, more so even than the tactile aspects which have so often been praised for their reality-value. The lion is not touching the sleeper—intangibility forms part of the general intransigent quality of things in Rousseau's paintings—but nor is the lion smelling her, which raises doubts about his predatory senses. What brings him hither? The answer presumably lies in the mandolin: the lullaby which the solitary woman in the desert sang to herself was enticing enough for the lion to come calling—now that St Jerome, whose iconic attributes had included the pet-like lion, was no longer around. In his case it was the aura of being pleasing to God that had kept the lion at heel. In the case of the sleeping woman, it is the absence of scent. The song has died away and not even the smell of prey remains in its place, for evidently the putative Gypsy has no scent. This is reflected as disappointment in the lion: no music, no meat. Perhaps it would not be too far-fetched to invert the usual interpretation of the image and propose that the sleeping woman has been dreamt up by the lion, and that in the dreams of lions there can even be Gypsy women who don't smell of anything.

All that is lacking in the moonlit desert must, by contrast, be there in abundance for the *hungry* lion, who, having just brought down his prey, is on the brink of satisfying his voracious appetite and enjoying a bloody feast beneath the carefully chosen exotic trees. And yet this lion also makes a rather disappointing impression, as if the artist had proscribed any demonstrations of unchecked voracity amid the delicately arranged jungle. If the dreamt-of or dreaming lion was disappointed in the Mooress because she had no smell, here the jungle predator is disappointed because his prey has no flavour, because it is under the curse of aesthetics. There is a hidden justification for the designation *The Hungry Lion*, for he is depicted at the precise moment when he would be certain of satisfying his hunger, if it weren't for the disruptive power of taste-subtraction. Thus he must go on being a hungry lion, prevented by the scenery that frames his performance from savouring his meal. This exacts an apostrophe: two years before his death, the tax collector-turned-painter is said to have been granted his most ardently desired accolade. Picasso, the only painter whom Rousseau considered his equal, held a banquet in his honour.

Rousseau's impeded lions are not a case of aesthetic amputation. The magic spell that binds them makes these lions representatives of the secret theme that unites almost all the works of this Sunday painter, who, after taking early retirement, would also paint on weekdays, but the spirit of the times would not allow him the freedom openly to declare his master idea: he was painting Paradise. Of course, it would not suffice to deduce this from the impeded lions, who seem to be placed there in contravention of the 'struggle for existence'. But Paradise is by definition the place in which lions are least able to be what they are while at the same time they cannot be allowed to suffer on account of their inherent leonine nature. This paradox requires only that the medium between things be lacking, which is what, in Rousseau's paintings, imbues things with that magical irrelationality: they have no atmosphere and no connection to other things. This means that in general, not just for the lions, nothing smells of anything and everything tastes of nothing. This is also why people who cannot find anything that is to their taste tend to like to imagine Paradise, either the one that is lost or the one that is to come.

When art historians speak of the 'archaic, magical thingness' of Rousseau's paintings, they are highlighting an antithesis between the thing and the world which has its mythical equivalent in the assertion that Paradise is not a world. On the contrary, it excludes or closes itself off from the world. The isolation of things—which in the realm of the ritual and the sacred is one of the most ancient practices; in aesthetics, however, a modern invention—imbues them with that which, in the web of the world and the haze of reality, they cannot have: an aura. If something smells of nothing and tastes of nothing, it can at least potentially claim auratic status. This is a rather unexpected form of 'transcendence', which even at that time was beginning to seem implausible. The one lion's indifference to the sleeping woman, the other's distaste for venison, their mutual animal inexpressiveness; it is all the expression of a withdrawal from the world which then comes to be described as 'archaic' or 'magical' but which ultimately refers to the quality of the 'thing' as that which is least accessible. In this case, no 'thing' has anything to do with any other, because they do not exist in any medium or on any ground that might be able to transmit that quantum of pheromones from one to the other. The lion is as far removed from the sleeping woman as the full moon in the desert sky, she is as unattainable for him as each leaf and each blade of grass is for the other in the paintings with the lushest flora.

It is the emptiness of the space between things that keeps their 'purity' inviolate. These things are not in the world; each is a world unto itself. Between them: *intermundia*, absolute delimitation from everything. This state of affairs, that things are not in a world, is so alien to our experience, so unimaginable, that we keep this surprise at bay by calling it archaic and magical.

The impeded lion's constitutive impediment is his unbelonging to a world in which it would be possible to get a close enough look at his mane, to look him straight in the eye, to see how 'artificial' they both are. He may not be able to smell anything, but he makes up for it by not letting it show.

## ONE SPECIES OF LEONINE ABSENCE

Ever since the end of feudalism, the hunting classes have consistently employed such excellent arguments in defence of their noble pursuit that to an impartial observer it can start to seem that they do protest a little too much: where, after all, have people ever been motivated purely by such lofty goals as stewardship, husbandry, conservation and love, when at the same time they each carry over their shoulder one of the most effective instruments of murder ever devised? We cannot reconcile words and appearances here any more than the critics and opponents can.

Despite my extensive engagement with everything relating to leonine absence, I was nevertheless unfamiliar with the lion story that Odo Marquard recounted during a lecture he gave in Berlin in 1983, to illustrate the situation of the sceptic. The sceptic, Marquard observes, is enamoured of the metaphysics that produces so many answers that they neutralize one another, reciprocally, so that ultimately the problems are left open just as they were at the start. The fate of such a sceptical amateur in metaphysics, he continues, is like that of the lion-loving lion hunter who, when asked how many lions he had already brought down, had to confess that the answer was none. To which he received the consoling response that, when it comes to lions, that's already a lot.

Can even an absent lion be a trophy? In his conclusion, Marquard suddenly, though not gratuitously, applies this anecdote to his favourite topic: theodicy. This special branch of metaphysics has so far not found any answers to the problem of God's justification for creating the world as it is. *But for human beings, that is already a lot*—that is the philosopher's final word.

As a sceptic, I am hesitant to endorse this scepticism unhesitatingly. It reminds me too much of another neat philosophical maxim: Philosophy is too hard for human beings. He who said it gave up philosophy and became an irenologist. Not that peace was any easier for human beings, of course, but it was in greater demand. Such statements too easily invite an implicit corollary that is fundamentally at odds with philosophical scepticism: too hard for us human beings, but God will know the answer. Surely, He must know the answer to the basic question of theodicy, namely: Why is there something rather than nothing? Otherwise, why would He have risked creating the world in the first place?

Here a sceptic must unflinchingly reply that God cannot answer the question any better than a metaphysician of the species *Homo sapiens sapiens* because the problem applies equally to Him as it does to the world: *Cur aliquid potius quam nihil*? Why does the Creator of the world exist rather than not? Just because He has been defined as *causa sui ipsius*?

Could, or rather should one not have told that lion-loving lion hunter (also by way of consolation) that he had spent his whole life hunting lions in a place where there aren't any? *Cur potius leo quam nequaquam?*

## ECCLESIASTES' DEAD LION

The author of the *Qōheleth* is what one might call the Schopenhauer of the Old Testament. And the same fate that awaited that grim dispraiser of existence among his colleagues in the academy also befell this collection of axiomatic wisdoms among the sources of Biblical Christian revelation authenticated by the Holy Spirit: there was reluctance to accept this sort of complacent affirmation of the negative as the Word of God. And so this book was cited even more selectively than the others, and the rest was left to the secular aphorists.

Why should God have felt the need to inform, or even just to remind, mankind that a living dog is better than a dead lion: *melior est canis vivens leone mortuo*, in the canonical language of the Vulgate. Surely this would make sense only within some heretical undercurrent that sought to exclude from Paradise certain predators and venomous animals that pose a threat to Man, so that the treacherous serpent would have had to have slithered through a gap in the fence surrounding the Garden of Eden in order to reach its goal. But if the pacified lion was also excluded, then why not the domesticated wolf? Could God, in accordance with His revelation, have accepted such a distinction in the value of the death of his creatures, whether they had been present in the Garden of Eden or not? But there is another, far more serious aspect: Ecclesiastes, the pessimist, does not consider life to be preferable to death. Life is subject to the oft-cited verdict of *vanitas vanitatum* from the first utterance. The corollary to this is bitter enough to warrant the general preference for the dead over the living: *Et laudavi magis mortuos quam viventes.* And even better off than either are those who were never born: *et feliciorem utroque iudicavi, qui necdum natus est, nec vidit mala quae sub sole fiunt.* This is the theodicean scorn of Attic tragedy.

The Biblical dictum, which would seem to betray the sorry truth of its author, occupies an Aesopian horizon: it could at any moment turn into a fable. The blustering lion, the humiliated dog, who promptly turns out to be the lion hunters' tracking hound, and who delivers this piece of wisdom just before the hunted lion breathes his last. But what would be the moral of the story?

We may come closer to finding the answer to that question if we consider the later use—or, rather, misuse—of the Biblical Preacher's phrase. In his *Life of Samuel Johnson*, published in 1791, James Boswell recalls a discussion at the Literary Club on 3 April 1778 involving, among others, Edmund Burke and Edward Gibbon. The topic was the exorbitant price of a marble statue, ostensibly of Alcibiades' dog. Johnson immediately knew how one might ascertain the dog's identity: 'His tail then must be docked. That was the mark of Alcibiades' dog.' This dubious verification could not quell Burke's outrage at the price: 'A thousand guineas! The representation of no animal whatever is worth so much. At this rate a dead dog would be worth more than a living lion.' Which clearly, to this well-versed company, would contravene the wisdom of Ecclesiastes—not to mention that of Plato, for whom representations are in any case inferior to the original Forms, to say nothing of representations of representations, if we assume that this marble portrait of 'Alcibiades' dog' was itself in fact a representation of an arbitrary exemplar of the species. For Johnson, however, the sculpture is not primarily a representation of some 'thing' but, rather, a testament to the artist's 'skill', which permits us to ignore the object of representation altogether. And nor is it simply a question of aesthetic authorship: 'Every thing that enlarges the sphere of human powers, that shows man he can do what he thought he could not do, is valuable,' declares Johnson, giving the example of the first man to balance a straw upon his nose—a court jester, in other words. Boswell attempts to halt the slide into redundancy by insisting that the worth must at least partially lie in the object, which must serve as a didactic criterion to discourage 'a misapplication of time and assiduity'. Addison, he notes, 'commends the judgement of a king, who as a suitable reward to a man that by long perseverance had attained to the art of throwing a barley-corn through the eye of a needle, gave him a bushel of barley.' To which Johnson mordantly replies: 'He has been a king of Scotland, where barley is scarce.'

If we consider how this debate on the fundamental questions of aesthetics relates to the Old Testament proverbialist, we see that Burke in fact takes that latter at his word while at the same time allowing a Platonized

disdain for the merely lifeless image to seep in sublimi-
nally, whereas Johnson's position is in line with that of the
Biblical author with respect to the glory of all of creation:
The dog, simply by virtue of being a creature of God,
must be equal to the lion, ergo a living dog is worth more
than a dead lion, which has only its appearance in its
favour. For *life* is precisely the highest quality and testament to the skill of the maker.

In the preface to his novel *Fräulein Rosa Herz*, Eduard
von Keyserling likewise makes use of Ecclesiastes' dictum.
The novel's heroine, he writes, is a poor, insignificant girl,
whose fate in itself is hardly remarkable enough to warrant
the telling. But such coyness is in fact designed to draw
surreptitious attention to the very 'skill' that Johnson,
more than a century before, had identified as the deter-
mining factor. Except that here the benefit is reserved
exclusively for the reader: in addition to his own life experience, the reader may come to know another life, assum-
ing the author has succeeded in bringing this poor,
insignificant girl to life in his novel. It is not a question of
pitting the living dog against the dead lion but, rather, the
life which the reader can experience versus that which may
remain unattainable for him—for whatever reason, but
perhaps first and foremost because he is himself a poor
insignificant fellow, one of many. 'Vitality'—the quality
of being alive—is the only 'quality' that may be given and
received and that would permit other, homogeneous lives
to be added to a life. And in that case, it makes no difference whether it is the life of a king or that of Rosalie, the
ballet master's daughter. The moment has arrived in

which the author can end on a proper, Biblical note by invoking Ecclesiastes' dog; what the dead lion lacks lies in the hands of the author's life-giving 'skill'. Yet, only in extreme circumstances, or so he seems to imply, would Keyserling have attempted this with a lion. Paradoxically, the thrill of demonstration is diminished when it comes to lions; it is simply easier to imagine a lion as being alive, as the stuffed models for the lion paintings at the salon in the previous century have shown. Thus, the Old Testament preacher does not even provide a lesson in humility—for that, it is far too easy for the modern aesthetic consciousness to compare itself to the Creator.

## THE ABSENCE ABOUT THE LION: MORGENSTERN

Christian Morgenstern's six-line poem 'The Lion' goes as follows:

A leaf of a calendar on the wall
displays a lion, grand and tall

He views you regal and serene
the whole of April seventeen

Reminding you, lest you forget,
that he is not extinct as yet.

Like the saints, who, due to their great and ever-growing number, were each allotted but a single day of the year, the calendar lion leads a diminished existence. Not even the guarantee of returning annually on the same date, such as the saints enjoy, is granted him: picture calendars have to be more varied than ecclesiastical years.

Nothing remains of the omnipresent threat which the lion of the Biblical world brought with him, and which made it logical to compare the Great Deceiver to a roaring lion, who walketh about, seeking whom he may devour (*leo rugiens quaerens quem devoret*). We do not think of him whenever and wherever we lay our heads to rest—we need to be reminded. One day a year for the lion—a tiny bit of presence in the middle of a far greater absence.

## THE ABSENT LION

Fontane's daughter Martha (Mete), concerned that her father is losing all his mirth in his old age, sends him a 'school scene' to cheer him up—*Teacher: Name 4 animals in Africa. Pupil: 3 lions and 1 rhinoceros*. Fontane passes the joke on to his old friend Georg Friedlaender, with whom he has spent many a vacation, adding: *I find it really first rate; in general, I value such indefinable jokes most of all*.

A mere dunce? At first glance, the joke seems quite straightforward: the boy employs a cunning ruse in order to disguise his ignorance of African fauna, for which he cannot be faulted because formally, at least, he has answered the question. Such characters are ten a penny.

But we might also imagine the pupil, consumed by the figure of the lion, thinking he is free to weight the specified number as he sees fit: the landscape is populated by a threefold lion and a singular rhinoceros—all the others 'don't count'.

But the indefinability of this 'school scene', which is reason enough for Fontane to pass it on to the earnest county judge, may also reside in the implicit reaction of the spectator, the observer. He sees the boy's enthusiasm for lions and knows Fontane as a proponent of the maxim, 'in for a penny, in for a pound'. The boy stops short of going all in; he lacks the courage to take the next logical step and answer: four lions! The indefinability of the joke is also this indefinitiveness which leaves open the exponential decision to allow everything to be dominated by the lion.

The pupil was one lion short of the triumph of the species.

Editions of a living author's complete works: that was an indulgence which hardly any publisher at the turn of the last century bestowed upon mere mortals. Nowadays, ever-younger authors are permitted to release their 'collected works', just as long as there are enough for more than one volume.

On 31 October 1897, Henrik Ibsen signed the contract for an eight-volume edition of his complete works with his German publisher Samuel Fischer. As ever disposed to hectic reception, Germany was the country where his influence penetrated deep into the public consciousness. The first volume was set to be published in Berlin in time for the playwright's seventieth birthday in 1898; at a time when his *Samlede verker* were not available even in the original language. There were numerous complications, particularly with regard to copyright, so the publisher was only barely able to get Volume 3, at least, on shelves by the appointed day. The Freie Bühne association, whose private performances of Ibsen's dramas had played no small part in spreading the word about their acts of liberation (because the appearance of exclusivity unfailingly gives rise to the paradox that everyone wants to take part), sent out invitations to a celebratory banquet. Max Liebermann, who was not a member but whose wife Martha was a great supporter of the naturalist avant-garde, was commissioned to demonstrate his congeniality with the guest of honour by decorating the menus.

The pen-and-ink drawing for the cover depicts an old-fashioned folio bearing the author's name, but prudently omitting the volume number from the spine, at the foot of which lie three not-altogether-fresh-looking laurel wreaths as a token of esteem. The monolithic dimensions of this singular volume can be explained by its static function as the pedestal for a monument: on the top edge lies a lion, forepaws sticking humbly out over the spine, and whose docile face, framed by a carefully coiffed mane, is that of the playwright himself. However much or little joy Liebermann may have taken in his task, he certainly makes it obvious, or at least makes no attempt to disguise the fact, that *ferocity* is no longer the emotion of the day when it comes to this lion perched on top of his bibliographic pedestal. A lion of resigned conviviality has been invited to an entirely bloodless 'feast'—that is the message.

Theodor and Martha Fontane were also members of the Freie Bühne. Fontane, who would not live to see the end of this jubilee year, was an avowed 'Ibsen enthusiast', with the proviso that he preferred Gerhart Hauptmann —and with the most stringent objection to the lifelessness of Ibsen's characters, above all that 'ninny' and 'chatterbox' Nora. In his view, while Ibsen had undoubtedly caused a stir in and around the theatre, he had done so by inadequate means.

What Ibsen, like all the other 'realists', lacked was something Fontane considered to be essentially 'realistic', namely, humour. Had he lived just a little longer he would have witnessed his most immediate successor adding precisely this ingredient to his *Buddenbrooks*.

Ibsen had the requisite earnestness without which presumably no one can achieve or maintain cult status. At the very end of his life, Fontane began to have misgivings about the 'cult of Ibsen' and in Hauptmann he found a suitable antidote. He could not have known that the same thing would happen to him as well. His prognosis for Ibsen, as he wrote to Paul Schlenther, was that in thirty years *tops* he would have *succumbed to comedy*. This was practically his final word on the matter, reiterated two days after the banquet: *I stand by that statement*. And the reason? The lack of the exact thing which he was supposed to have been the first playwright to have brought to the stage: *Everyone keeps blathering on about Ibsen's truth, but I maintain that truth is precisely what he lacks*.

Nevertheless, as he affirms in what would be his final comments on the playwright in May 1898, Fontane's opinion of Ibsen as the great *reformer of the stage* who had created new figures and *above all, a new language*, remained *practically unchanged*. The fact that many of his characters were stock figures shouldn't be held against him. In the end, there is his legacy, arising out of a certain commonality in the biographies of the playwright and his critic. And this truly is the final word Fontane had to say about Ibsen: *In the end he was . . . an apothecary*.

This digression from Liebermann's menu to Fontane's final verdict has been more than a gratuitous apostrophe to Ibsen's contemporaries. For that which Liebermann

would fail, almost demonstratively, to deliver in his leonine portrait of Ibsen, in 1896 he had already presented
Fontane with a tribute to veracity: *Days of sittings, days of
painting*, as the impatient author had described the
prospect of having the artist extract his likeness. Precisely
because the subject matter was not a 'lion' but, rather,
the zone of indeterminacy between reality and humour,
the blurring of all physiognomic contours in old age, it
was a singular task for this subverter of the conventions
of portraiture. The 'preliminary' chalk sketch for something that was never 'finished'—and which now resides
in Bremen—is the treasure in which, in a different way,
the finale of *Der Stechlin* has been preserved for us.

The viewer also has reason to feel he has been preserved. Preserved from a lion.

Readers of the New Testament apocrypha, the books not incorporated into the canon of Holy Scriptures, particularly the large number that have been discovered since 1945, may be disappointed by the theological poverty of the contents, by the tawdry thaumaturgy, especially on the part of the Apostles, by the garrulousness of the narrators, but they will nevertheless be rewarded for their pains in one way at least: their admiration for the selection process that led to the establishment of the core collection of canonical texts. On the whole, good taste, a sense of the tolerable and the judgement of theological substance have decided fairly unerringly. How fortunate for the latterday reader of the Bible that the *Acts of Peter*, for instance, notwithstanding their enormous popularity, have not been canonized. People are forever dying and being resurrected left, right and centre! These *Acts* also contain the famous question 'Quo vadis?', which was likewise lost, and has survived only thanks to the novel by Sienkiewicz.

The *Acts of Paul* seem only narrowly to have missed out on canonical status. If they hadn't, we would have been given the third letter to the Corinthians. But the surviving fragments give a clear indication as to why they failed to be canonized: the baptism of the lion. It is still possible to cite the resistance such an expansion of the sacrament encountered. Another singular episode is one in which the virgin Thecla baptizes herself in the arena where she has been set upon by wild beasts; in the name of Jesus Christ she throws herself into a pool full of seals. The story of Thecla revolves around the repeated preservation of her virginity, and is thus perfectly consonant with Paul's preaching, whose central message is sexual abstinence and very little else. This is also the reason for the persecution he suffers: The man is making our women aloof and recalcitrant! If it weren't for that no one would have had any objections to him. At the end of the second century CE, when the *Acts of Paul* are thought to have been written, all other aspects of Christianity seem to have been forgotten: Salvation lies in sexual abstinence, and this message appears to have been enthusiastically received, above all, by women. They are the executors of the Apostle's orders, and the men were out for revenge.

In Ephesus things have once again come to a head. The local goldsmiths throng the governor Hieronymus: *To the beasts with the man*! A foretaste for the prisoner Paul is the sound of a lion roaring so fiercely that even the apostle, hardened to such things, *breaks off his prayer in terror*. When the assembled spectators hear the roar, it is not just *a* lion but, rather, *The lion*! And: *Come let us see the man who possesses God fighting with the beasts*! The Governor himself now runs into trouble with his wife Artemilla, who has spent the night before the spectacle praying with Paul in his cell. Luckily, they have only recently captured a *very fierce lion*.

The confrontation between the lion and Paul in the arena is a decidedly civil affair—even if the fragmented text, as it has come down to us, may not preserve all the pleasantries: *But the lion looked at Paul and Paul at the lion.* They recognize each other: *Lion, wast it thou whom I baptized?* At this, the modern reader of the *Acts of Paul* in the venerable edition of the *Acta apostolorum apocrypha* by Lipsius and Bonnet is likely to be perplexed, for he knows nothing of such a backstory, a *Historia Pauli et Leonis*. It was generally assumed that after his Damascene conversion Paul must have met the lion on the road to Jerusalem and baptized him. For how else could the wild beast in the arena have responded, *Yes!*, with typically leonine laconicism, to the question posed by his designated victim? Even more wonderful than this terse answer is the next, when Paul asks the lion how he came to be captured, to which he responds: *Even as thou, Paul.* There is more that links them than baptismal water; this is the fellowship of prisoners.

Not until the discovery of a Coptic papyrus in 1959 did we learn more about this baptized lion. Here Paul recounts to his audience in Ephesus how once, after his conversion, he had been approached by a *great and terrible lion* who came *out of the valley of the burying ground*. But the lion had given the lie to his terrifying aspect and thrown himself at the feet of the new convert. Even then, their conversation had been brief: *Lion, what wilt thou?* Paul had asked. And the lion had replied: *I wish to be baptized.* Paul, as he goes on to tell the Ephesians, had not made things easy for himself with the lion. He had raised his voice to the Heavens, to Him who had shut the mouths of the lions with Daniel, but opened the mouth of this lion to express such a pious desire; next he had stepped into a nearby river, taken the lion by the mane and immersed him three times in the name of Jesus Christ. Together they had come up out of the water, the lion had shaken his mane and bid farewell to his baptist with a *Grace be with thee!*, to which he had replied, *And likewise with thee!* And that was that.

The Apostle has just one more detail to share about this lion: after his baptism, the lion had come across a lioness but had not so much as looked at her. Instead, he had run off. This may be laying it on a little thick, but it is perfectly in line with Paul's general tendency, according to this 'Encratitic' source. In the case of this lion at least, the manifest success of the baptism was that he was clearly no longer prepared to propagate his glory.

Thus, if we may group this Coptic papyrus with previously known fragments of the *Acts of Paul*, then at least some of the faithful Ephesians who witnessed the events at the arena will already have suspected what the story was on this lion and how he had wound up in this unfortunate predicament, his terrible ferocity notwithstanding. The organizer of this spectacle, Hieronymus, whom Paul had deprived of his conjugal pleasure, suspects nothing and invites further misfortune.

The fraternization in the arena, and the absence of the lion's promised ferocity, make the Governor impatient, and he orders more wild beasts to be let loose on Paul, and archers on the lion. At the sight of such unsportsmanlike

behaviour even Heaven is enraged and decides to inter-
vene with a violent hailstorm. The other animals are
struck dead by the hail, and Hieronymus loses an ear,
preparing him for kindness at the hands of the unresentful
miracle-worker at a later date. *But it did not touch Paul or
the lion*. Without another word—everything had been
said—Paul bids farewell to the lion and makes his way
to the harbour and boards a ship bound for Macedonia.
The harbour is full of people fleeing the city, certain
that it will be destroyed. Saving oneself from impending
doom has always been a favourite occupation of human
beings—and what more can you really do for yourself
besides saving yourself from impending doom?

The fate of the lion finds final expression in a single
sentence, which is worthy of the majesty of this animal,
baptism notwithstanding: *But the lion went away into the
mountains, as was customary for it.*

For one single soterially indispensable moment only
had he interrupted the consummation of his nature.

Regrettably, the *Acts of Paul* also tell us something
about the Apostle's exterior. The canonical scriptures—
to their infinite advantage—do not breathe a word about
Jesus' outward appearance. But the loquacious chroniclers
in 200 CE cannot leave any aspect of their pious readers'
curiosity unsatisfied. In Iconium, a man by the name of
Onesiphorus sees Paul, whom he knows only from Titus'
description, coming towards him on the royal road to
Lystra: *a man small of stature, with a bald head and crooked
legs* . . . The reader would do well to have forgotten this
information by the time, much later in the text, he is called

upon to imagine Paul and his baptized lion meeting face to face in the arena in Ephesus. Can we still understand the stuffy critics who begrudged a lion his baptism, when, with such dignity and decorum, he had turned away from this single absolution for his ferocity and gone back into the mountains—henceforth, presumably, to be even wilder than before?

## THE RENEWED ABSENCE OF LEONINE THOUGHT

The lion, having for a single moment in the history of his species been granted the power of thought, was forced to recognize, much to his chagrin, that he was not the supreme hunter on his prey's feeding grounds. They were all faster than him. They disappeared over the savannah as soon as they caught wind of him. He could not hunt whatever he wanted. He merely took what the herds of antelope and zebras left behind, the weakest and most decrepit of their number, the ones that could not keep pace with their mocking elusiveness, the ones that fell behind the rest.

Then the lion immediately gave up thinking and instead left hunting to the females. Thus, gradually, his equanimity returned, which in years to come would be interpreted as regal lethargy by visitors to the lion enclosure at the zoo, and which stood in such irresoluble contradiction to the myth of the lion's wildness.

Man, by contrast, from the very first moment of his history as a species, having been pushed out of the increasingly sparse tertiary rainforest, had been obliged to face the sobering reality that his strength and speed were inferior to anything on the savannah which he would have to hunt if he was to survive. Hence, he could afford neither to renounce thinking nor to spurn it.

And so he invented the prototypical concept: the trap. It is the realization of thought in the compact sense: a device whose application, arrangement, suspension and retrieval allow someone absent to make something absent his prey. The trap is cognitively matched to the prey for which it is set: its shape, its strength, its behaviour and its movements. Whoever is better at thinking catches more prey.

For the hunters of the species *Homo sapiens* there was no reason to leave the hunting to someone else. While the trap lay in wait, they were lying with their women in the cave and enjoying the previous catch. Did this make them into patriarchs? Not quite. For they were still dependent on the praise and favour that only the proper thought of that which was absent, the successful application of the concept, could provide.

The first Schopenhauerian to be made professor of philosophy in Germany was Paul Deussen, a childhood friend of Nietzsche's from the days when even he did not yet despise Schopenhauer's ubiquity of the 'I' in everything else. That had changed by 1887 when Deussen, en route from Kiel to the Mediterranean, stopped off in Sils-Maria to visit Nietzsche.

Little is known about this last meeting of theirs, but it must have been as fruitless as it was brief. And the story of the Buddha which Deussen recounted to Nietzsche, having come across it in the course of his Indological studies, following up on Schopenhauer's leads, cannot have contributed to the strength of their friendship. It is one of the great narratives for the promotion of pensiveness, if I may put it in such old-fashioned terms.

Buddha encounters a hungry lion. In order to satisfy his hunger, he changes himself into a rabbit. To the follower of Schopenhauer, this was still a permissible miniature: even though it was a lion and hence a product of the Will in one of its purest forms, Buddha's compassion is still great enough that he cannot disdain his hunger; and yet he does precisely that when, in recognition of that hunger, he turns himself into an offering of the smallest quantity of meat imaginable, little better than nothing at all when it comes to satisfying a lion's hunger. Despite the Buddha's metamorphosis, the lion will have continued to feel the lack and turned his thoughts from rabbits to other sources of nourishment.

Nietzsche will hardly have regarded his friend's story as a gift meant to satisfy his intellectual appetite for recognition and fealty. He had long despised any sense of sympathy for hungry lions. Why were they hungry? Because they had failed to make anything of their leonine courage. A starving lion did not deserve even a rabbit. He deserved to starve.

Was Paul Deussen perhaps thinking of the ruthlessness with which his friend had once urged him to *strip off the theological bearskin* and to *act like a young philological lion*? Now, there was the lion, but he was hungry, and had had to make do with this sympathy-rabbit.

## THE CARES OF THE LIONESS

There are not many poems more ubiquitous and well-known than 'The Panther' from Rilke's *New Poems* (1907). There is—at least for people living within a certain historical proximity—such a thing as too much success: the more familiar a cherished object becomes, the more its attendant aesthetic quality is erased. Franz Marc's animal paintings, loved by an entire generation, would suffer a similar fate: they became worn out, rather than outworn. It was not until *The Tower of Blue Horses* went missing, probably for good, that people suddenly experienced the shock of realization that the existence of this work of art, famous to the point of satiation, was anything but self-evident. Poems by contrast cannot be lost for ever: their presence is not diminished by reproduction, regardless of what may have happened to the autograph manuscript. The original may be infinitely rare but that has no impact on our ability to experience the work itself.

The gaze, grown weary from the passing of the bars of the cage at the Jardin des Plantes, for which there is no meaning to anything outside this enclosed space—'no world' beyond the 'as if' of the 'thousand bars'—grounds the panther's inner concentric motion, the 'dance of force around a centre' which, to the eyes of the visitors, appears empty but which nevertheless keeps those 'powerful soft strides' in orbit, just as the centre of gravity of the solar system keeps the heavenly bodies in motion. The poet is unlikely to have had Schopenhauer in mind when the empty centre of that gravitation appeared to him to be inhabited by a force which he likens to a 'great will' that has been 'numbed' by the smallness of the space to which its influence has been reduced.

Dated that same summer of 1907, there is a 'reoccupation' of this central motif from 'The Panther' to be found among the brief suite of *Prose Poems*, which begins with 'The Fishmonger's Stall'. Compared to that Neapolitan gem, 'The Lion Cage', written as early as November 1902, is by far the lesser work. Nevertheless, it is important in relation to that moment in the composition of 'The Panther' that one might call the 'contingency' of the poem: the evidence of its necessary haecceity emerges out of the ground of a possible alterity.

The disquiet of the lioness in her cage differs from that of the panther, because she is not alone. She is circling the male lion, and the lion is sick. It is not a 'force' that keeps the lioness in orbit but, rather, a powerlessness that must be cared for: as if her care had been translated into a circling. What drives her is not a will that can be numbed by the space, but, rather, her memory, as if captivity were the cause of her companion's sickness—the interchange of captivity and inner turmoil which she, with her memory, appears to want to drive out: *Being sick doesn't concern him and doesn't diminish him; it just hems him in*. Yet she cannot take the knowledge that her memory offers her and turn it into a cure: she doesn't have a poem.

He doesn't *have* the memory; he *shows* it as that which he lacks. He is a monument, *erected upon himself in memory of his own mourning*, of the absence of what he once was: *the exaggeration of his strength*. He is not a lion on the verge of dying of homesickness because it is his companion who carries that nostalgic longing for him. He is a creature of futility, and he celebrates it as if it were a ritual. The internal twitch of a muscle; the enclaves of anger; the blood bursting from the chambers of his heart, rushing to his brain: all these are mechanisms of a suddenness that has lost its meaning. Only the signs of his contempt for his current state are meaningful, the tiny gestures of wildness renounced—a renunciation of life itself perhaps, if life could be killed by contempt. At just such a sign the lioness stops her endless circling and sees with alarm and expectation how he himself no longer wishes to be that which is happening to him: *Only far off, as though held away from himself, he paints with the soft paintbrush of his tail, again and again, a small, semicircular gesture of indescribable disdain*. At this, the sick lion's guardian resumes her *desperate, ridiculous pacing*, and, like a sentinel, *falls back into the same tracks, again and again*.

*She moves the way clocks move*. Here, in this single phrase, which would not be out of place in a non-prose poem, the difference between the lioness and the panther is clearly accentuated. It is not the bars of the cage which prevent her from preying on the outside world. Hers is not a tamed centrifugality but, rather, the self-restraint of care, the steadfast physiognomy of dependability in that *terrifying hour, in which someone dies*. But death, in the mutual indeterminacy of resignation and renunciation, marks an absence about the lion: the appearance of that which is to come, the illusion of care, the indifference of what will actually happen. For in this leonine memory death does not appear; just as in 'The Panther' the 'great will' had grown numb, here death is the blindness of a care that cares for nothing.

## THE FEARFUL LION

People have never really been able to agree on a definition of progress—either in a positive or negative sense—nor even on what such a definition might potentially look like. Anyone hoping for consensus on the matter is in for a long wait. There is *one* point on which there is widespread agreement, however: Progress means increasing permissiveness. The criterion being that the people of the past, or those who dare to go on living, take on the whiff of prudishness. And yet they are completely indispensable: Who else is going to be shocked by this new licentiousness?

When the times are changing, no one wants to be left behind. Least of all those who cannot come along. A keen-eyed memorialist describes the upheaval after the First World War: *One thing is for certain*: *Nobody wanted to appear old-fashioned*. A conservative art critic, no longer young and only moderately reconciled to the avant-garde, had unexpectedly married a young girl and transformed his Eliza into an exotic beauty. She bore him a child, and the word around town—and an uncommon word at that—was that this was an *umbrella baby*.

A term which, unlikely as it may seem, finally brings us to the promised lion. This bourgeois utensil serves as a prop in a little joke about a man walking through the desert. Suddenly, a lion appears. The man is startled and opens his umbrella, presumably in order not to have to look at the lion any more. But the result is that which the magical act of shutting one's eyes has always promised since time immemorial, and particularly since childhood: the lion falls down dead.

Someone else had shot the lion at that exact moment.

It seems like a bad pun when we learn that the aforementioned critic, who by this detour was in pursuit of modernity, had elected to focus his unwavering eye for backwardness on a particular playwright by the telling name of Lion. Late in life, the latter's widow, Marta, recounted this story of surpassing progressiveness. Even those mistrustful of the reminiscences of widows, because of their notorious vindictiveness, will be able to appreciate the applicability of this fable to any and all gaps in time.

## THE DREAMT-OUT DREAM OF THE LION'S ABSENCE

In 1902, Romain Rolland wrote his pacifist drama *Le temps viendra*; in 1921, the critic Alfred Polgar saw a production of it. By then, Rolland had been vindicated in his premonitions and condemnations of war, but to Polgar what he had imagined now seemed like *such a darling little war*, that the whole thing was reduced to *story-book magic*.

Even the ending, where the *good soldier* stands over the dead body of the *good general* and speaks the title phrase: 'The time will come.' By which he means the messianic time announced by the Prophet Isaiah, when *the lion will lie down with the lamb*. To the critic, this prognosis has been definitively refuted; not least because, as he observes, the lion has never had anything against this arrangement. *What are true prophets good for?* he wonders, concluding that the only beneficiaries are the prophets themselves, whose fame is secured in the moment the catastrophe they prophesied comes to pass. *We are beyond help. The time will come when the lion will lie down with the lamb, you say? Maybe so. But then the lion's claws will have fallen out, or else the lamb will have grown some.*

Polgar would reprise this review, published in the *Weltbühne* in 1921, almost verbatim, when, in February 1936, he was asked by the *Prager Tagblatt* to honour

Rolland on the occasion of the lifelong pacifist's seventieth birthday. Not that there is anything wrong with him referring back to his 'final image' of the lion and the lamb's role reversal—but it does highlight the unbelievable duplicity of a situation that now makes it necessary to blame the pacifist for the unavoidability of the next war. The play, once again declared obsolete, now testifies to the *hopelessness of human affairs* rather than to the hope of the messianic age to come. And the whole thing now bears the title, 'Are prophets good for anything?'

In 1925, Polgar happened upon another play by a right-thinking pacifist, *Heinrich aus Andernach*. In his review, Polgar describes the playwright, Fritz von Unruh, as *an enthusiastic advocatus agni*, adding that writers were just as capable of empathizing *with lambs as with lions*. But, he writes, even more bitterly than four years earlier, *in any given situation, including that of Germany, it is irrelevant whether the lamb is willing to leave the lion lying next to it in peace*. This is the peacetime poetry of the defeated. They look to the lamb, not the lion. He is not there: *for this regal beast, alas, no more parts are being written*. The political disaster is also a *calamity for the theatre!—They would be putting on different plays by the Rhine today if history had taken a different turn*. Then at least there would have been parts for lions!

In 1932, we have Julius Hay's *Das Neue Paradies*. By now it has become an either-or proposition: in the state of grace, either the lion will have lost his claws, *or else* the lamb will have to have grown some. The playwright has made his choice—his comedy makes the case for the only viable option, *viz.* the latter. This new paradise, an abortive fantasy, leaves the lion as he is and advocates instead for the armament of the lamb, as a deterrent to lions who might want to eat it.

## IN DEFENCE OF THE ABSENT LION

Wittgenstein's notes from the years 1941 and 1944, posthumously published in Part 5 of his *Remarks on the Foundations of Mathematics*, contain one of his explicit 'retractions' of the *Tractatus*: *In other words, my conception is a different one here*. At issue is the lion as a fable animal and the question of whether statements about him—in other words, those found in the genre of the fable—fulfil the criterion put forward in the *Tractatus* that they have sense. Without doubt the fable lion is an absent lion and hence is not part of *everything that is the case*, i.e. the 'world' as defined in the opening sentence of the *Tractatus*. The lion in fables is not the species *felis leo*, nor is he an individual by the name of Leo. In fables, *the* lion goes for a walk with *the* fox, *not a lion with a fox; nor yet the lion so-and-so with the fox so-and-so*. And yet it *actually is as if the species lion came to be seen as a lion*. Even if you give the lion the name 'Lion', Wittgenstein continues, explicitly contradicting Lessing, the principal theoretician of the fable, *it isn't as if a particular lion were put in the place of some lion or other*.

If these suppositions are eliminated, the fable lion is in danger of being banished to the realm of nonsense, in accordance with the law of the *Tractatus*. Can it really be that fables, these little distillations of significance—indeed what is often considered their most ancient form—should meet such an end? One is tempted to say that it was for the sake of the absent fable lion that Wittgenstein retracted the rigorism of his definition of 'sense' as the representation of the world. *Even though 'the class of all lions is not a lion' seems like nonsense, to which one can only ascribe a sense out of politeness; still I do not want to take it like that, but as a proper sentence, if only it is taken right. (And so not like in the* Tractatus). . . . A 'proper sentence'—that sounds more like Lessing than logic in the context of the *Tractatus'* requirements for proper worldliness; and hence it requires that this lion, absent from the world as he is, must nevertheless appear 'in something', and thus represents a new and different type of 'case': *Now this means that I am saying: there is a language-game in* this *sentence too.* While he may not appear in the world as such, he does appear in *one* of the language-games of the world's name-givers, and that is what brings the absent lion back to existence and to life. It is a magic wand, or else a formula for licenses.

For instance: *Imagine a language in which the class of lions is called 'the lion of all lions'* . . . . *Because people imagine all lions as forming* one *big lion. (We say: 'God created man').* And yet we cannot help but imagine him as a particular lion and, moreover, one that bears the name of his species. This procedure, which seeks to recuperate fables and creation myths, inevitably leads to the dreaded paradoxes Bertrand Russell warned us about. *Then it would be possible to set up the paradox that there isn't a definite number of all lions.* Which would be plainly nonsensical in a world in which everything that is the case not only 'exists' but does so with the necessary attribute of existing as a definite quantity. Nothing that is supposed to 'exist' can be permitted to lead us to the impasse of having to insist on an indeterminacy of its quantity. But it is entirely possible that this is exactly what the fable is seeking to do.

Wittgenstein is an heir of Socrates', not least in his cunning use of counter questions as a means of getting out of such difficult situations. In response to the example proposition, *The class of cats is not a cat*, he quite unprofessionally asks: *How do you know?* Would the answer not have to be: Because that would lead to a contradiction?

Which brings us to *the* critical point where we can almost hear him say: 'So what?' But does he say it for the sake of the lion? I would like to believe that he does, but I cannot. For professional reasons, for the sake of my reputation. Unfortunately, it is not worth breaking the philosopher's oath for the sake of a lion in a fable: contradiction must be avoided at all costs. Hence for Wittgenstein too there must be something 'higher' at stake. For instance, that we cannot afford to preclude or to forfeit entire realms of possibility simply because we cannot conclusively stave off the distant threat of contradiction. What separates the philosopher of the 'language-game' from the entire philosophical tradition, including his teacher Bertrand Russell, is the 'frivolity' with which he invites the objection and the threat of contradiction and disregards the obligation to prove non-contradiction, in the interest of saving 'what we can quite easily live with'.

It is here that the precision of Wittgenstein's examples reaches its peak. He draws a comparison with the 'certainty' of the banking system, to which he, having willingly divested himself of his paternal inheritance, no longer has recourse: *What sort of certainty is it that is based on the fact that in general there* won't *actually be a run on the banks by all of their customers; though they would break if it did happen?*! *Well, it is a* different *kind of certainty from the more primitive one, but it is a kind of certainty all the same.* What a crash course in monetary theory, especially considering that even in this century a logically serious system was completely focused on the apocalyptic possibility that all deposits might be withdrawn in a *single* day! Wittgenstein's example serves to postulate that the utmost degree of certainty is insufficient reason to suspend an ostensibly humane institution until it is able to meet the last requirement of certainty: *I mean: if a contradiction were now actually found in arithmetic—that would only prove that an arithmetic with* such *a contradiction in it could render very good service; and it will be better for us to modify our concept of the certainty required, than to say that it would really not yet have been a proper arithmetic.*

Even if Wittgenstein does not say this for the sake of the absent lion, nevertheless this is what saves him: We can continue to write fables about the lion without fear of falling into the nonsense trap laid out by the *Tractatus*. The thinker's leonine courage.

Hence: What are we to make of the philosophical advice—good or bad—that we must live with the possibility that there is an unresolved contradiction at the bottom of one of our 'language-games', or perhaps in more than one, perhaps even in all of them? It must be regarded as a sophisticated piece of Cartesian provisional morality. Not: 'This far and no further!' but rather: 'Until further notice!' But we must take another look at the one dispensing this advice. As is so often the case, it is the perfectionists who, having known the disappointment of not living up to their own demands, produce the most compelling formulae of resignation as the human variant of perfection. It is their suffering that lends these formulae credibility: the passion of asking too much of oneself. This is what unites Wittgenstein's *Tractatus* with his 'retractions' in such a way that it becomes impossible to speak of a 'conversion' or a 'turn' with any pathos or reproof. Even if Wittgenstein had not foreseen that he would be forced to withdraw his earlier claim.

Which of course ran utterly counter to his furious personality. A brief anecdotal clash recounted by his Russian teacher Fania Pascal gives a sense of the air of blunt rigorism that he continued to project long after his philosophical revision. In the summer of 1937, Wittgenstein made the two 'confessions' to his closest friends which have baffled his biographers. Having recounted the second of these to Mrs Pascal—like the first, it turned on an untruth; in this case, his having denied an act he committed during his brief tenure as a village schoolteacher in southern Austria—she was astonished not because of the lie but, rather, by the reason for which he felt compelled to own up to it a whole decade after the fact: *What is it? You want to be perfect?* she asked. Whereupon he had pulled himself up proudly and said: *Of course I want to be perfect.* It was this scene in particular that made Pascal *burst with the wish* to write down her memories of Wittgenstein. I cite it here not in order to demonstrate Wittgenstein's Kierkegaardian talent for guilt. Rather it is a question of how un-self-evident it must now appear to us that he should have relaxed the genuine rigour of his perfectionism with respect to the threat of contradiction. And yet even if, out of a sense of guilt—however slight this time—he had in the case of the absent lion disputed the ancient fable's right to exist with the arrogance of logic, it would only have been pro forma.

Perhaps, in order to express what lies in the irresolubility of the threat of contradiction, one would have to do so in the manner of Plato, in the form of a myth. There is one singular moment where Wittgenstein specifically signals just this: namely, when he writes god in the plural. *The contradiction*, he writes, *might be conceived as a hint from the gods that I am to act and* not *consider*. On those rare occasions when he speaks of God and not of the gods, the predicate is different: God *shows*, He does not hint.

## DELAYED EFFECTS OF ABSENT LIONS

The fact that the citizens of Zurich wanted a zoo like the Baslers had to do with the absence of the lions that the Negus Negesti of Abyssinia had given to the city at the end of the first decade of the twentieth century. At that time, the lions had had to be sent to Basel for room and board, owing to the lack of suitable quarters in Zurich. Understandably, it gnawed at the Zürchers' pride to have to go to Basel to see their lions. But Zurich had always been circumspect with regard to unnecessary expenditures, even though experience had repeatedly shown that even the ostensibly necessary ones rarely prove their worth in practise.

And so it was not until 1929, on 8 September, that the *Neue Zürcher Zeitung* was able to announce, under the somewhat rose-tinted headline 'Patience Rewarded', the opening of the zoological garden. The lions, however, who had been on loan to Basel, and who could be said to have initiated the idea, were not present for the festivities. First, because they no longer numbered among the living inventory of the Basel zoo; and second, because the city's frugality meant that although a stately carnivore enclosure at the edge of the woods was clearly visible on the panorama drawing that accompanied the newspaper story, the fine-print caption was obliged to point out that this section of the park—and, as if that made it better, also the bear compound—would be added at a later stage of the construction.

The people of Zurich's intimate affinity with the lion did not find adequate expression until June 1986, when the eighth annual Zurich Tourism Prize, funded by the Swiss Bankers' Association and the tourist office, was awarded to the 'Zurich Bahnhofstraße Association' for their campaign to decorate the Bahnhofstraße with lions. Of course, these lions were made of plastic and had been commissioned from a factory—a 'studio-factory', rather, to be precise. The window dressers from the associated businesses were involved in the visually striking installation and decoration, and the whole thing turned out to be an 'outstanding tourism event', according to the jury's statement. Now, if the 'lion fancier' mentioned in the 1929 newspaper article found himself seized by the 'urge to conduct research' which it likewise discussed, he would have been able to satisfy that and various other desires in the Bahnhofstraße. How much money they could have saved in 1929 if only they had already had the idea, the 'studio-factory' and the plastic by then.

For in order to do something prizeworthy in those days, the lions would still have had to be made out of bronze.

## THE ABSENCE ABOUT THE SEA LION

What kind of leader was the Führer? Any attempt to answer this question invites the suspicion of wanting to dispense with, and thus trivialize, the problem of responsibility for deeds and misdeeds. But this is a misapprehension, which arises from the historical observer's own susceptibility to the suggestive power of the image the Führer sought to project of his 'leadership': namely, that he was the incarnation of concentrated will which in turn supplied his qualification to lead.

It would likewise be wrong to say that the Führer delegated leadership to others. What he did largely leave to others was the work of making him the leader. The procedure can be reduced to the following formula: For those whom Hitler had selectively chosen as his inner circle, it was more important to know the will of the Führer than to carry it out. And to know Hitler's will meant being certain at all times what he would want before he had even willed it.

Nor did the executors of this will simply invent actions which they would have to carry out, and then ascribe them to Hitler after the fact. But there is something to the notion that they tried, above all, to foster his assurance that it had all been his will and that he had thus been in command. At the same time, he was not the sort of man who lets others foist their will upon him. What he was supposed to have willed had to correspond to the implied intent of his actions and to be inherently indistinguishable from that which he would have willed to be done, had he had the opportunity to will it. The pseudo-genius of his Paladins-elect consisted in 'being able to tell' how he would lead so that they could allow him to be the leader. It was the explication of his implications. He who was most 'faithful' in this regard was rewarded with divinatory influence which he could then dress up in the uniform of unwavering loyalty and orderly obedience. Himmler was constantly in the business of formulating Hitler's dreams for a distant future after the great victories had been won. And yet he was not the master diviner; that title belongs to Goebbels, who showed no signs of such utopian distance, always appearing as the man who enabled the Führer to meet the demands of the day. Others were specialists in presumptive obedience through planning and conceptualization. Through Speer, Hitler dreamt of immortality.

Above all, the title of 'greatest commander of all time', which had been invented by Keitel following the victory in the West, actually referred to the product of his predictive counsellors. If the defeat of France had not been the work of his generals or even his authority but, rather, his 'genius', then he must also be the one who knew how to move forward to the final, definitive victory. His admiral Raeder dreaded the next step, the inevitable 'directive' ordering him to cross the Channel—and did precisely that which prepared the way for what he wanted to prevent: he examined all the options for an attack. Chief of the

Army General Staff Halder could not imagine that the Führer had been unprepared for the swift defeat of the French and had no discernible plans for what would and should come next. The Army competed with the Navy and the *Luftwaffe* in anticipatory planning, preparation, exercises and resource allocation for an operation that could not fail to take place, for which they expected to receive the order and the timeline any day—just as the British on their island were waiting day and night for the invasion. One might think that there was simply no one who dared to *say* out loud that Hitler did not know how to proceed; the truth, however, is that it never occurred to anyone to think such a thought. The divinatory mechanism appeared to have broken down. Who imputed to Hitler what his 'genius' ought by implication to have coughed up? In fact, the real reason the wild improvisations from the Netherlands to Brittany had proceeded at such a pace was that they had wanted to be prepared for the incalculability that is a hallmark of genius: a state of heightened receptivity set in. There is no record or report of Hitler uttering a single word on any of this.

Almost no attention was given in these calculations to taking stock of what the German military had and what they might realistically achieve. Mostly, they were exhilarated that at this moment and under these conditions and this Führer 'everything' had become possible. Already preparing his memoirs, the Panzer strategist Guderian wrote that during the night of 20 May 1940 a battalion of the Second Panzer Division had reached the *Atlantic coast* at Noyelle. This, presumably, was the misjudged sense of proportion that had got the staff's brains all in a whirl running through every conceivable plan in order to demonstrate the exorbitance and hence impossibility of this undertaking. But on the other hand, was exorbitance not precisely to be expected?

Hitler was confident that he had a rhetorical solution to this and other problems: *We will come to an understanding with England*—on 17 June this was still his proposed solution, as he informed Göring, who would receive the most thankless task in the invasion, namely, the battle for air supremacy over the landing area, and who was the least disposed to worry about taking stock of what he really had and estimating what he could really achieve. He let the others do the guesswork and simply declared that he could do everything that was required of him.

Within a few days the conjecture had become the manifest product of the Führer's will, who had up until then been entirely will-less. On 11 July, the Grand Admiral visits Obersalzberg to report on the possibility of an invasion of England. Hitler, already at work on his 'big' Reichstag speech, has no difficulty conceding that this should only be seen *as a last resort to force peace on England*. Apart from that, they indulge in visions of building the German fleet after the final victory which will make Germany a *first-class oceanic naval power*. On 13 July, Halder arrives to present his invasion plans. Hitler remarks that he has no interest in dismantling British world power, whose successor would be America. But on 16 July, Hitler issues Directive No. 16, ordering preparations for a landing operation in England, code name: Sea Lion.

On 19 July, Hitler gives his speech extending the 'magnanimous' offer of peace to England. It proved as ineffectual as Directive No. 16. They had all guessed correctly all the same.

## THE POLEMICAL LION

You don't have to be a conservationist to see that a world
without lions would be a dismal place. Even though, after
Schopenhauer's disappointment at the lack of elan exhib-
ited by the lions at the Berlin zoo, and subsequent devel-
opments in the science of ethology, the nimbus that once
surrounded the heraldic king of the bestiary is all but
gone—and, needless to say, it was the indolent male lions
whose regal manes were most diminished in the process—
nevertheless, it will be a long time before such demythol-
ogization has any real impact on the physiognomic
impressions made by childhood visits to the zoo and the
circus. That is, if there is any reason to believe that scientific discoveries have any influence on our own perception
of the world. The sun still rises and sets, after all.

The notion that lionesses are not simply bound to give
birth to lions, but obligated to do so, is a sub-genre of the
polemic. In Aesop's fable, the lioness, mocked by the
pluriparous vixen for having only one cub, responds with
unalloyed pride: *hena alla leonta*—Just the one, yes, but
he's a lion! The corollary being he had better grow up to
be a lion worthy of the name.

I have begun to wonder whether this 'natural' state of
things, elevated to a norm, has been beneficial to our
literature. Recent discoveries about the lethargy of lions

might have put a timely damper on their polemical misuse.

One particularly egregious instance is Heinrich Heine's *The Baths of Lucca*, where he enlists the help of some lions to vent his (and their) spleen on August von Platen. The lion is meant to demonstrate to him that a young poet is not allowed to refer to works which he may compose in the future—that hope is not a credible principle. Rather, he must be at once all that he can be: *The lioness does not first bring forth a rabbit, then a hare, then a hound and finally a lion*. Which is not only self-evident, it is just one of the inanities of this desultory and hateful tirade.

Any imaginative credibility is jettisoned in the non sequitur of the following sentence which, instead of comparing the poet to the lioness in terms of his poetry, casts him as her firstborn cub, even though she neither wrote him like a poem, nor had to be a lion herself in order to give birth to him: *Madame Goethe, at her first birth brought forth her young lion, and he in turn gave us his lion of Berlichingen*. The poet cannot rely on showing 'promise' in his works—at most there may be the promise of more polish, more refinement, more maturity to come. This is why Goethe was 'allowed' to write *The Natural Daughter* and Schiller *The Bride of Messina* only *after* having written *The Robbers*: *whose claws at once showed the lion breed*.

Count Platen's beginnings, by contrast, were altogether un-lion-like, and marked by *anxious and elaborate art*. Perhaps it might be objected that before Dostoevsky's

*Crime and Punishment* no one could have known how narrow is the gap separating animalization from murder. But in Heine's diatribe something has been set in motion that could breed dragons rather than lion cubs, as a passage a few pages after the leonine insult reveals. In order to justify the elaborate acerbity of his dissection of the Platen phenomenon, Heine has recourse to science: *Everything is of importance to science*, he writes, and so, by implication, the pursuit of the truly important justifies whatever means facilitate it. Hence: *let him who would reproach me for devoting myself too seriously to Count Platen go to Paris and see with what care the accurate, exquisite Cuvier, in his lectures, describes the filthiest insect even to the minutest particulars.*

There is no clemency to be had here. We are not far from Raskolnikov's old pawnbroker, who deserves to be deprived of her worthless, verminous existence in the name of a sublime higher purpose. Here we can see how important it is to be a lion from the start—not because the proper way of the world demands that wildness come before domesticity (just as genius must come before urbanity) but, rather, because it makes one less likely than this insect to become a target for Cuvier's and Heine's lectures; an insect whose designation as *filthy* makes no sense from either an orthodox or a secular perspective—except as an incitement to its extermination.

I do not think that one should take such irresponsible utterances lightly, given that a century later their author would himself have been hard-pressed to save himself from the unfortunate stigma of not having been born a lion but something else entirely. Heine merely considered it aberrant not to be a lion, or not to have become one in time. He could not have imagined how dangerous it was merely to cast doubt on such matters.

## THE PRESENCE OF A LION—AS IF HE WERE ABSENT

The view of nature contained in the creation myth at the beginning of the Bible is a mere short story compared to the cosmology propagated in Psalm 104. God's creation of the world had been a show of force that could inspire the weak-spirited through the ages; and his government of the world so great and praiseworthy that it impels the cry of: *Bless the Lord, O my soul*. He who made the light likewise makes the darkness come again, *wherein all the beasts of the forest do creep forth*—including the young lions, who *roar after their prey* and look to God for sustenance like every other thing. But when the sun rises anew, they make themselves scarce and lie down in their dens. For the daylight is made for man alone: *Man goeth forth unto his work and to his labour until the evening*.

Commentators have never been content to stick to the text itself, however apparent its meaning. Not only did they add their own material, they also had their own rival theorems. The exegesis of Psalm 104 in the Midrash Tehillim contains the fable of the three carnivores: the lion, the wolf and the dog. Once upon a time, when they all happened to meet, the lion tried to attack the dog. Then he saw the wolf, and because the wolf was yellow, which must have seemed uncanny to him, he grew afraid and abandoned his prey. What he did not know was that the yellow wolf, in turn, was afraid of the dog. Which reveals just how unfamiliar his domesticated cousin had become. The experience of mutual fear enables the three to coexist in peace: *Thus the three creatures did no harm to one another.*

This must have made a greater impression on Rabbi Akiva, who witnessed the encounter, than what the Psalm itself has to say about the symbiosis of lion and man. For it is not the Lord's benevolent sparing of the workers in the field that causes him to utter the accolade in the next verse of the psalm but, rather, this fear-bound trinity before his eyes: *How manifold are Thy works, O Lord! In wisdom hast thou made them all . . .*

Rabbi Akiva was one of the participants in the last Jewish revolt under Bar Kokhba and was executed by the Romans in 135 CE. The enrichment and systematicity in the interpretation of the Law, and hence Talmudic method, were established by him. Like many others, he regarded Bar Kokhba as the Jewish Messiah, but this error has not been held against him. What his animal fable makes abundantly clear, however, is the way his faith in the world order differs fundamentally from the Psalmist's. His is not the divinely decreed order of classifications and allocations, of collision prevention; Akiva's natural order emerges immanently. The lion is not absent so that the others may live; he is both present and ravenously hungry, but even he has a fear that prevents him from satisfying his every urge and desire. This order is that of an equilibrium of fears. And thus an *indirect* expression of divine wisdom.

For *this* theologian it is sufficient that peace be the result of fear and not of love and tenderness. When would lions ever have loved what they could eat if they did not fear something else? Absence or fear, that was the alternative of theologically inspired wisdom. Everything else is just morals.

## THE REMEDY FOR THE LION'S RETURN

The young doctor has assumed the duties of his father in the latter's small-town practice that serves the surrounding countryside, while his father is realizing his dream of practicing in the big city for a few more years and putting his renowned pulmonary treatment to the test. But soon after he is suddenly taken ill and, at the urgent advice of a colleague, the son must go and fetch his father, before he has had the opportunity of making his beautiful expectations a reality.

For his father, the train journey from Munich to Passau is like 'Purgatory', and he hovers on the edge of consciousness, until, shortly before their arrival, a small boy in their compartment bursts into bitter tears, and his mother tries in vain to comfort him. Guiltily she explains the calamity to the young doctor. At home in Plattling, she says, the boy's uncle had mentioned a stone lion that could be seen from the train between Seestetten and Schalding, gazing from its lofty pedestal over the Danube valley. Hans Carossa knew the local landmark well, having grown up near Seestetten; in fact, he had only just caught sight of his mother and sister stepping out of the door of his parents' house. But the boy's mother had been mistaken about which side of the train would afford a view of the granite monument to King Maximilian. And so the little boy had missed the lion, and for the mother it was no small thing to have revealed herself to be ignorant of such a matter.

But was it really important enough for the author, one year before his death, to recall this scene from over half a century before, and to devote a page to it in his memoir, *The Day of the Young Doctor*? Neither the regal lion nor the child robbed of its aspect by a directional mix-up are the 'carriers' of this memory; rather, it is the father's brief emergence from his lethargic state. One last time he *laughed as in days of good health* and even proved the master of the situation, as the experienced therapist, ready with a coin for the boy and *instructions* for the mother regarding which side of the train to spot the lion from on their return journey, *lest the misfortune repeat itself* . . .

At this point in the narrative, the reader is already familiar with the conflict that informed Carossa's early life: his loyalty to his father and the medical profession, versus his plans for a writerly existence. The absent lion was just an occasion for a final reminder from a father to his son that he should appreciate and take into consideration when deciding on his future that people are creatures in need of consolation, and that a doctor's job is not least that of knowing how to provide that consolation and reassurance.

We understand: it had to be a granite lion in a river landscape in order to render the child's expectation and disappointment emotionally palpable; but at the same time the peculiar comedy of disproportion which had expressed itself in the ailing doctor's laughter—who had immediately known the perfect remedy for the deficiency. A scene of leave-taking and obligation, far below the threshold of pathos.

## SEA LIONS——A MISUNDERSTANDING

Before life in the course of its evolution came on land and made itself visible, the most difficult transitions and leaps of its precarious beginnings beneath the surface of optical conspicuousness, in the seas and oceans, were already behind it. Occasionally, it has gone back there. As the great marine mammals did—to their later detriment. For only in the sea could they achieve the necessary quantities of flesh and blubber to make them irresistible, almost to the point of extinction, for large-scale human alimentation —think: 'margarine'.

Only rarely does this return to the sea assume the character of a demonstration. The Moscow newspaper *Pravda* permitted itself to indulge in its newly increased freedom when, in May 1987, it published a story on a state circus that had staged an unusual publicity stunt. In Sochi, on the shore of the Black Sea, the trainer instructed his troupe of sea lions to demonstrate the tricks they would perform in the show. The stunt proved effective. Soon a crowd had gathered and the circus seemed assured of a healthy take at the box office that evening, that is, if the sea lions hadn't thought better of the proposition and instead made a break for the open sea, never to be seen again.

They had an advantage over their unrelated terrestrial namesake when it came to disappearing from view. The lion also has his absences, but he lacks a dimension that would allow him to absent himself voluntarily. Thus he remains the king of the jungle, but also of the circus.

### THE LION'S ABSENCE FOR THE ELEPHANT

Man is the animal that keeps other animals. Domestic animals, at first, and then, much later, display animals.

With regard to the latter, there is a clear preference for two species in particular, so much so that any menagerie —or zoological garden, as they're now called—without them is basically invalidated. You can't have a zoo without lions and elephants. When it comes to everything else, people are quite tolerant.

It is notable that these two animals mostly leave each other alone, despite the fact that the one is notoriously carnivorous while the other is decidedly carniferous. At the same time, one cannot truly say that they live together in peace and harmony and that it is this which man likes to see on display.

If they leave each other alone, it is not out of mutual affection. At most, one might say that it is out of mutual indifference.

This indifference is the most solid foundation for their survival. Compared to that, any and all forms of 'love' must appear dangerous. Food for thought for those who are not content simply not to let anything happen. The only thing safer than saying that 'nothing *must* happen' is to say that 'nothing *can* happen'. And for that, the safest condition is the state of affairs that obtains between the elephant and the lion: the one is absent for the other.

## THE ABSENCE ABOUT THE LION:
## ST JEROME IN HIS STUDY WITH AN HOURGLASS

The church father Jerome, whose remains are said to be interred in Santa Maria Maggiore in Rome, was embroiled in all the major dogmatic disputes at the turn of the fifth century. Although he had studied rhetoric, his ascetic fervour would frequently drive him into the desert for long periods of silence. To be sure, he would then return at regular intervals with large quantities of writings. This idiosyncrasy of his stringent asceticism is rendered visible in the configuration of *St Jerome in His Study*: the writing hermit with the desert lion as a pet infected with piety. The viewer is bothered by the harmlessness of the lion on panels and woodcuts, for they do not reveal how such a symbiosis came to be in the first place.

The Schnütgen Collection in Cologne contains a wooden sculpture from the early sixteenth century, where the lion is still wild and dangerous, poised to pounce on the Saint but held back by the latter's posture which is equal parts rhetoric and devotion. And so perhaps it was out of gratitude for having been deterred from sancticide that the lion took up the task of guarding the hermitage, to ensure that the theologian would not be bothered by any other beasts of prey.

The persuasive force of this interpretation derives from rhetoric, which can subdue even the wildest opponents, but also from the scholar's need to keep 'reality' close at hand, albeit with a softened temperament. This lion, as the great Biblical scholar well knows, is still the roaring lion of the Psalms who walketh about, seeking whom he may devour. And yet it is the same word, which, in that image, represents the adversary of man, which, in the guise of rhetoric, has the lion eating out of his hand.

Rhetoric and reality: this confrontation, transformed into a configuration, renders *St Jerome in His Study* eternal, recurring in ever-new 'reoccupations'. In his *Hourglass Book*, Ernst Jünger presents the opposition between abstract, mechanical time as embodied in the rigour of clockwork, and natural, elemental time as embodied in the measure of the hourglass. A variation on the Romantic alternatives to all mechanical 'driving forces', leading us *to the gate of timeless gardens, where no hour tolls*. This is so seductive an idea that time and again we are almost inclined to give credence to it—just as to the hermit and the lion. Jünger, who is referring to Dürer's 1514 etching with the hourglass between the galero and the skull, likewise employs powerful rhetoric in his text which raises questions that require no answer: *Who wouldn't want to partake of this stillness, amidst that warm wooden panelling, while in the corner the sand trickles through the hourglass and before the desk a lion lies dreaming, for which one might easily substitute a cat?* The ending is disheartening and duplicitous: if this is meant to be a Hieronymic icon, then the lion cannot be replaced by any domesticated feline, even if, beside the sleeping lion, Dürer has placed a pet dog, likewise asleep: a bourgeois idyll. But would it still serve as proof of the power of the word that emerges from such a hermitage, if that word had not yet overpowered crude reality in the form of its royal representative? Metaphors that take such turns are not to be trusted.

## CONCILIATORY EXPULSION OF THE LION

There are no lions in the land of Canaan any more.

A Midrash Tanhuma explains how this came to pass. One day, Rabbi Hanina ben Dosa encountered a lion. He knew from the fables that he was the king of the beasts. But what did he care about fables? So he shouted at him: *O you weak king! Did I not adjure you long ago never again to show yourself in the land of Israel?* The lion must have forgotten, since upon being so forcefully reminded he immediately fled.

For what follows, psychology is the wrong discipline. The Rabbi runs after the lion, catches up with him and says: *Forgive me for calling you weak when He who created you called you mighty. For it is written: 'The lion, which is the mightiest among beasts.'*

The legend does not tell us what happened after that. In any case the lion remained absent from the land of his dispraisal. Not because the apology was not accepted but presumably because this reprimand had been preceded by the adjuration never again to show himself in the land of Canaan. The Rabbi did not retract any portion of that. It had been a test of strength, and he had won. Was he justified in reprimanding this lion who—as if this were already the Messianic Age—was obeying his command?

But it is not remorse for this act that caused the Rabbi to run after the lion. He had been thinking of the fables, and in that light it was easy to make fun of the one who could not resist the reprimand. But once the lion's physical presence had already been negated, the Rabbi, well versed in scripture as he was, must have remembered what it says in the Proverbs, and hence the word of Him who knows more about lions than any Rabbi. To have contradicted Him—that was bad. It was the Creator on whose behalf the Rabbi apologized to His creature.

And yet: Was this—that the lion is the mightiest among beasts—a reason not to let him feel the might of man, and indeed to expel him from the land with an adjuration?

Since then, there have been no lions in Canaan. Reconciled, and yet banished, they make the land Promised through their absence.

The moral reprehensibility of the lie is one thing, the liberating power of the truth is another.

If lying is impermissible, one can nevertheless get by because while one should of course always speak the truth, not everything that is true must be spoken. The permission to remain silent guards against the various difficulties that may arise from the prohibition against lying.

But if truth is linked to freedom, then it must be forbidden to keep it back. It is astonishing to observe the persistent association of the truth with the promise of freedom, although this presumption has disappeared from the scientific conception of cognitive truth. Above all, Freudian psychoanalysis is founded on the unacknowledged principle of the liberating power of the truth, more specifically, reflexive truth. One must steer *oneself* towards one's *own* truth in order to liberate oneself from 'unfreedom', which is what every psychological anomaly is in its essence.

It is curious to see how this elementary idea, which arose from the *intentio obliqua* of self-analysis, came to be extrapolated as a political maxim for use against *other people*. We are told never to keep silent if we know the truth. This is nothing other than an attempt to save an absolute for the cause of immanence: in the consensus of everyone about everyone which in fact turns out to be the consensus of the few *against everyone else*, we find the familiar pathos of the preacher of repentance, whose cry of *metanoeite* [*repent*] also serves to exempt the one who utters it from confessing to the state of his own affairs. Rhetoric as a tactic for self-preservation.

Luther held Aesop's fables in high esteem, second only to the Bible, and considered them, together with Cato, to be *meliora omnium philosophorum* . . . One of his favourites was the one about the lion's den. The lion was wont to invite the other animals into his foul-smelling cave and then ask them how they thought it smelt (*quomodo oleret*). The wolf said bluntly: 'It stinks.' The ass, sycophantically: 'It smells good.' The fox equivocated: 'I've got a cold.' Luther has no qualms about supporting the morality of this answer: *Non ubique omnia esse dicenda*! It may be a lie, but it is assumed that the lion will readily understand it as a firm refusal to provide an answer: 'I've got a cold, *id est, non licet quaecunque dicere.*'

Fortunately for our moral impartiality, we do not learn what the lion did with those who refused to affirm the fragrancy of his den. The fox's shrewdness merits a *non licet* simply because as a guest one abides by the rules of politeness prohibiting one from uttering anything derogatory about the host's domicile.

That said, *this* is not the truth that sets you free; for that, Luther has a dependable alternative. But for those who don't, another will have to do—at a pinch the truth about oneself.

Myth tells not only of terrors that have occurred in the past but first and foremost *that* they are *in the past*.

In Thebes lay the tomb of the king's daughter Semele, whom Zeus had impregnated. Even the still-smouldering bedroom in Cadmus' palace could be seen, where Zeus had fulfilled his promise to reveal himself to his lover naked and in his true form—Hera having contrived to plant seeds of doubt in Semele's mind as to whether Zeus truly was the father of her child, the unborn Dionysus. The old thunder god's fiery nature could no more forestall the consequences than nakedness in general can curb its effects: Semele perished in the flames of her beloved and at that very moment, terrified and thunderstruck, gave birth to the god of self-forgetting, whose character was in keeping with the circumstances in which he came into the light of the world—a world to which he was destined to bring so much confusion. Are we allowed to be reminded here of Moses, who on Mount Sinai was not permitted to see the local thunder god Yahweh except from behind, lest he be struck dead by the *kabod* of the divine countenance, never to return from the mountaintop with the promised commandments? Whereas of course the Christians had always been taught that the promise of salvation was to sit eternally face to face in the blessed presence of their god. All blessedness hinges on the definitive end of terror.

Semele's tomb in Thebes is the setting for the greatest of all Greek tragedies, Euripides' *Bacchae*. It celebrates the fact that her death, brought about by the god stripped of his benign disguise, had been the final and definitive manifestation of his naked truth. From now on, the god must repeatedly demonstrate his goodwill towards this new and dependable world order by allowing the story of his discarded pasts to be represented.

But the account has not yet been settled when, at the beginning of the tragedy, Dionysus enters the Theban stage by his mother's grave: mothers, least of all if they are dead, are not to be appeased by the father of the gods simply putting a good face on things—even if his role in this had for once not been marked by falsehood. The doubt which Hera had kindled in Semele concerning Zeus' part in the conception has, following Semele's fiery death, spread to the city at large: Was this not in fact a dynastic trick on the part of her father Cadmus, who, in ascribing his daughter's shameful illegitimate pregnancy to the notoriously adulterous Zeus, was seeking to lay claim to a mythical consanguinity for his royal lineage? Dionysus is deeply chagrined by this calumny against his mother and his own divinity. He has succeeded in establishing a dubious cult around himself, full of intoxication and deceit and vulgar masquerade. As if he wanted to make a mockery of the divine privilege of metamorphosis, the gods' originary prerogative to assume any and all forms, by showing how this can also be staged as madness and delirium. Dionysus thus presents a parody of the Olympian pantheon. He is not a devil, but certainly an anti-god, who toys with his devotees, the Theban women whom he has goaded out of the city in a frenzy.

This alien god who roams the land spreading confusion is desperately seeking legitimacy by improving his mythical genealogy: he had been cast from the dying Semele's womb as more of a miscarriage, leaving him at the mercy of Hera's unrelenting jealousy; but Zeus had rescued him and sown him into his thigh, from which he had been born a second, indubitable time, as a bull-horned buck-god who would always have difficulty maintaining human form for the sake of the mission. It remains unclear where exactly he had come from when the women of Thebes followed him into the mountains seeking self-fulfilment; but it is intriguing to note that the list of potential points of origin corresponds exactly to the catalogue which had been proposed for Aesop, the father of the fable tradition: either Phrygian, Lydian or Thracian. Dionysus is aligned with Aesop because of his association with theriomorphism which he never quite overcame, bull-horned even at the moment of his second, Jovian birth (*taurokerōn theon*). More so even than anarchy and frenzy, it is bestialization that takes hold of his followers, the Maenads; they tear apart living beasts and eat the flesh raw, uniformed in the skins of fawns, their god's 'sacred garment' (*hieron endyton*). The myth itself tells of how the 'last' god of moderation in ritual, polis and cosmos gave birth, from his own body and as his legitimate scion, this adversary, who sweeps the Theban women out of the polis and into the mountains to the re-barbarization of *hunting the blood of the slain goat, a raw-eaten delight*. King Pentheus of Thebes perceives in all of this nothing but a case of mistaken identity: it is not Dionysus who is in control of this scene, he thinks, but Aphrodite.

In Aeschylus' *Oresteia* the last of the bloody rituals—the son's vengeance upon his mother for the murder of his father—had been brought to an end by Athena, the patroness of the city, establishing the rule of law and transforming the Erinyes into protectors of the legal order. Whereas in Sophocles' *Antigone* the parity between the earth's right to the bodies of the dead and the right of the polis to its hard-won laws had been shown to be a tragic and deadly parity for the antagonists. Now, in Euripides' *Bacchae*, it is the return of the anarchy of the alien god with the inversion of the bloody deed and its perpetrator which leads this triad of classical tragedy back to its starting point, and asks whether Agave's frenzied and thoroughly bestialized murder of her son Pentheus is worse than the act of filial vengeance for the death of a father returning home to his adulterous wife, which had been committed as the preordained consummation of an age-old pattern of 'restitution'. In Euripides's play, Pentheus' dismemberment at the hands of the Maenads is framed by a frenzied and bestial thirst for blood, animals against animals. Only with difficulty is Dionysus able to suppress the animal inside him until he has convinced Pentheus to disguise himself as a woman and go and see what's going on at Mount Kithairon. When they exit the city, the seducer is already horned, already the bull, an indication of his by-now untameable urge. But for Pentheus this is insufficient warning. It has become bad 'theology' when this lack of self-control serves to confirm the power of the god of intoxication, whom the Chorus declares to be *hēssōn oudenos theōn*. Through this return to the starting point and through the inversion of the poles of sexual dominance, the history of Attic tragedy as such has achieved mythic significance; and to regard this as anything other than the intended 'effect' would be to underestimate the artifice of this, the most influential of the tragedians. What makes Euripides close to the Sophists *and* to Socrates—a proximity that was thought to have been perceived early on—is the form of power which his god possess: he is the lord of neither the world nor the polis; he subjugates humans, above all those among them who are most susceptible to him, namely, women. His power is rhetoric, or a wild caricature thereof. Whether or not that speaks in its favour is irrelevant. What does matter is that once under the spell of this demigod (only demi-, for his grave will be placed in Delphi) who is hostile to any form of order, the King, on his way into the mountains, transposes the illusion of augmented power onto the city of Thebes, wrongly imagining that it will be to its benefit. The fallacy of anarchic salvation through bloodlust can only become 'political' if one does not enjoy the favour of feminine affinity to this god—bull or goat. 'Terrible' (*deinos*), that most polysemous of mythical attributes employed by the Greeks, which, in the comparative form, the Chorus in *Antigone* had already applied to mankind, will, in Dionysus' vision upon leaving the city, carry the cruelly ironic ambiguity of Pentheus' return in the arms of his mother Agave: his wretched voyeuristic debasement will receive 'terrible' punishment.

When Pentheus, having been ousted from his vantage point—which, in fact, proves disadvantageous in more ways than one—is torn limb from limb by the frenzied Maenads, he is no different from any of the other animals they have already dismembered. The cannibalistic culmination of the sacrificial rite fomented by Dionysus: *His mother, as priestess, began the slaughter, and fell upon him* ... Nor can he save himself by tearing off his disguise and revealing his identity. She skewers her son's head on the end of her ritual thyrsus, like the head of a slain lion which the returning huntresses parade as a trophy through the streets of the city. Is this just a metaphor? Hardly. It is a further ruse on the part of the seductive god, a piece of rhetoric made flesh, now aimed at the mass delusion of the polis itself. Just a few years before Socrates' death by poisoned speech and poisoned chalice (the tragedy premiered posthumously in Athens shortly before the turn of the century) this warning about the virulence of dehumanization went unheard.

Delusion—the constitutive form of fate in tragedy: *atē*, visited upon mankind by the gods—is, in this case, more than mere deception and something other than hallucination. It comes close to metamorphosis. It is not that Pentheus' head fixed to the end of Agave's thyrsus merely *appears* like the head of a lion; Agave has *raised* him to that status, in the words which the Chorus puts in her mouth in this strophe of the fourth stasimon: *he was not born from a woman's blood, but is the offspring [genos] of some lioness [leainas de tinos] or of Libyan Gorgons.*

The tragedy has a dual ending: on the one hand, Agave's awakening from her Dionysian madness and her delusion of having captured and dismembered a lion with her bare hands, whose head is now to be placed at the royal palace as a trophy, to the dismaying realization that it was her own son's head which she has carried with her from the mountains of Kithairon; and, on the other hand, the appearance of the *deus ex machina* above the palace roof, of Dionysus who proudly declares his vengeance to be righteous and sanctioned by Zeus, and goes on to hold court to banish what is left of Cadmus' family from Thebes. The presiding judge is the aggrieved himself, having avenged the irreverence he has suffered from the city that had cast doubt upon the 'Olympic' legitimacy of his conception and denied his 'dynastic' claim. Once again the tragic term *deinos* is used to describe that which the god now claims *ex cathedra* to have avenged through this murderous brutalization: *Yes, for I suffered terrible [deina] things at your hands, with my name not honoured in Thebes.* Once Cadmus and Agave have left the city along with her formerly Maenadic sisters, the Chorus impassively reflect that the gods meddle in the affairs of humans in many different ways—*pollai morphai tōn daimoniōn*—without the humans being aware of it: *aelptōs*. It is not just that they know not what they do, as Jesus will posit in their favour in his first word on the cross on Golgotha—no, here the god robs them of their sense of what they do, and of their right to know it. The alien god Dionysus, who forces his way into the Hellenic pantheon and turns this tragedy into a celebration of himself, is *diábolos* in every sense: the sower of confusion and the accuser, the obstreperous heir of the highest god demanding to be venerated and worshipped by humans, with the voucher of legitimacy—and even the judge in the tribunal that overturns the old order in Thebes, just as Aeschylus had had Athena establish a new one upon the Areopagus.

Euripides' *deus ex machina* not only superimposes this 'theology' upon the 'psychological' element of Agave's coming to her senses, it also removes any chance it might have had to serve as 'experience', as 'history', as any kind of salvation for the city of Thebes and the Spartoi dynasty—except perhaps the disaster of other royals' misfortunes being visited upon the polis. Dionysus too found a way to accomplish the unexpected; this is the Chorus' final 'great word' before they declare the matter closed (*apebē tode pragma*). In light of this moral about finding a way, it is striking just how excessive Agave's imaginary lion had been, what an elaborate delusion, as if it were the signature of a still-inexpert parvenu in godly matters, who still feels the need to be petty when turning down Cadmus' plea for forgiveness: *You have learnt it too late* [sc. *that I am a god*]; *you did not know it when you should have*. This is the fundamental formula of myth—as Goethe formulated it once and for all: *Only a god may prevail against a god*. The Thebans will have it hammered into them. Compared to that—and that was all they were supposed to know!—a woman tearing apart a lion with her bare hands is nothing, not even if it had been a real one.

## FELICITOUS ANIMAL METAPHOR

The proverbial lion's den is an ambivalent place: whoever enters is exposed to the greatest of all dangers; whoever is already inside (having failed to tempt the lion) is blissfully protected from any and all external threats. An impression that is reinforced by the ancient belief that the eyes of a lion are never closed.

In March 1989, the Historical Commission of the German Social Democratic Party (SPD) organized a conference at the Erich Ollenhauer House in Bonn, the party headquarters. The topic was 'forty years of the Federal Republic'. One of the panel discussions, regarding 'the democratic society of the future', saw Lothar Späth and Oskar Lafontaine, in their capacities as prime ministers of their respective states—and, presumably, also as aspirants to the leadership in their respective parties—in action. Afterwards, the gentleman from Baden-Württemberg is reported to have said: 'It was very convivial'—but then, was there any situation he would not have called convivial [*gemütlich*]? His statement was significant only insofar as the gentleman from Saarland had just informed him that he had arrived *in the den of the lionesses and the lions*. Where could he have felt more secure, once he was inside?

There is always a certain risk involved in invoking the major images of the rhetorical tradition.

None of which would be particularly remarkable if the deputy chairman had not subjected even this quip to the constitutionally mandated strictures of political correctness, differentiating between the male and female occupants of the proverbial den. This may well have been a first, and it serves as a link between fable and history. It had never really occurred to anyone that the classical lion's den should be regarded as a male privilege, rather than referring simply to the dwelling of the species *felis leo* which, in a manner both felicitous and rare, succeeds *grammatically* in uniting both sexes without, *in practise*, designating either the one or the other. Whether, in the face of the distribution of leonine gender roles, the man in the den would have more luck with male or female occupants is, in the case of this particular felid, difficult to translate into a bon mot.

Linguistically, the surrogate host had less difficulty than he would have, had he wanted to put his guest— incidentally: Where is a host to find a feminine form of 'guest'?—into metaphorical proximity to the stag, an animal of comparable mythological virulence. This animal, the most frequently represented in stone-age cave paintings and in the form of ritual masks, now inhabits the idiom of the *Platzhirsch*, or alpha stag, a paltry reminder of its erstwhile dominance. In that case the gentleman from Baden-Württemberg would have enjoyed a convivial welcome 'in the clearing of the alpha hinds and stags'. Unfortunately, however, the *clearing of Being*, like its guardian, had a very bad name at that time, and had thus become metaphorically unusable.

## TONIO KRÖGER'S LIONS

*There was the hotel, and there, reclining in front of it, were the two black lions he had feared as a child. They still glared at each other as if they were about to sneeze; only they seemed to have grown much smaller. Tonio Kröger passed between them.* And he will do so two more times in this novella. It is part of the 'test of courage' which he has set himself with this visit to his native city. Since his childhood, it has become a *cramped town*, just as the lions outside the hotel have grown smaller in the meantime. This had to do with his point of view, for unlike in his childhood, the guest was no longer forced to look up at the two lions flanking the hotel steps. They let him pass, even the third time when, paperless like a bohemian and hence not above official suspicion, he left the building to continue his travels. Did he still have *nothing but scorn in his heart*, as he had had when he first 'went forth' from this city, as the text somewhat grandiloquently puts it?

Not quite. He still has to confront his father, who has been stolen away by death and who had freely given him permission to leave, so the *scorn in his heart* was hard to justify. His hasty return, which was not supposed to be any sort of 'homecoming' and which would not spare him the tiny passion of being humiliated by the helmeted policeman Petersen in front of Seehase, the hotelier—

whom, like the lions, Tonio *knew by sight, from long ago*—
was just a *bizarre visit to his native town*. And this time the
city would not let him go without a fight.

When he had arrived with the aim of taking the ferry
north to the Danish seaside, there had been no indication
of any such difficulties. Ultimately, it was the indirect
result of a conversion: the negation of the opposite course
of action. He wanted to be certain that he was not heading
back south to Italy: 'Thanks, but no thanks,' as he had told
Lisaveta Ivanovna upon his departure from Munich. 'That
whole *bellezza* business makes me nervous.' 'I'm so indif-
ferent to Italy that I practically despise it.' On this first
stop towards his renunciative journey north, this too is
represented by the pitiful appearance of the two cast-iron
hotel lions, forever frozen on the cusp of a sneeze. And the
nervousness he felt in the South also had a counterpart
here: on his way to the 'grand hotel', which needless
to say was not located near the railway station, *nervous
laughter* had welled up within him, *a laughter secretly akin
to sobbing*. After thirteen years away, he didn't know
whether to laugh or cry upon seeing the 'tiny and crooked'
old town, where everything was *cramped and close together*,
the way life had tauntingly preserved and at the same time
erased it: *He was almost there*. Of course, there were lions
guarding the entrance to his destination, but Tonio now
walked straight past them like a man who can afford to do
so. This was something of an imposture on his part—in a
higher sense, of course.

Even though these once-fearsome lions now appeared
to lie at the guest's feet—I knew these lions well, and I

also know why they lent themselves so well to 'tests of courage'. For years I used to pass by them on my way to school. If I was not afraid of them the way little Tonio had been, it was not because I was the more courageous child. I simply did not see them as heraldic predators and sentinels but, rather, as animals waiting to be skilfully mounted, their backs rubbed smooth by generations of young riders. And the courage to be tested had nothing to do with their leonine nature and the terrifying expressions on their faces but, rather, with the ornately liveried figure of the hotel doorman, who himself guarded the guard lions and would not tolerate children sullying the prestige of his hotel with their mischief. At fairly regular intervals, which we always had to keep in mind, he would put an end to our games—though this was presumably ancillary to his main objective which was to keep a lookout for approaching guests. Of course, the miscreants themselves would never have accepted this; we preferred to see ourselves as the centre of attention. We knew from the reports of our numerous predecessors how to avoid the danger at just the right moment by sliding down the outer lion's flank and disappearing down the narrow alleyway towards St Peter's.

And so we probably had neither the time nor the inclination to notice that the lions looked like they were about to sneeze, not even that they were looking at each other. People never see the same things. To me their entire attitude was one of indifference, and I thought they were overlooking the fountain on the Klingenberg, which was always dry and presumably had been ever since the horse-drawn hotel carriages stopped stopping there. Even though it had run dry, that fountain was dear to me, and I missed it when, following the destruction of the bombing on the night of Palm Sunday 1942, it was suddenly gone—along with the lions. It was said that they had needed the metal for the war effort anyway. But that wasn't true; contrary to appearances, the lions weren't made of even semi-precious metal. This saved them from being requisitioned for any other purpose as well.

For no sooner had the city that Tonio Kröger so despised risen from the rubble—his author having contributed to the restoration of the seven-spired panorama—than the lions were back. Democratized, as was only fitting, they were now placed on either side the low, wide steps that lead away from the busy traffic around the Holsten Gate and down into the relative seclusion of the gently sloping park which leads through that famous gate, familiar from banknotes and marzipan, into the old town. If we imagine Tonio Kröger returning to the city, he would only have had to pass once by these good-natured lions which the police, too busy with the motorcars, now ignore completely. Hence, the lions could no longer serve as a leitmotif to mark arrival *and* departure, the crucial test, successfully passed and, in the interim, his morning walk to his father's house: *He ordered breakfast, ate, and went down, passed through the lobby, past the assessing glances of the desk clerk and the fine gentleman in black, and then between the lions and out into the open.* Where was he going? This question recurs three times. The first time the answer is: *He scarcely knew.* By the third it is simply: *Home.*

But at that very moment, he makes a detour outside the old city walls past the railway station and the Lindenplatz, and from there *through the old, squat gateway, along the waterfront and up the steep, draughty road lined with gabled houses, to his parental home.* If he were to return to the city, this particular detour would necessarily have led him past the two lions. Would he even have recognized them now, placed so far apart?

The temporal displacement implied in this question is not merely rhetorical. For we must now say a few words about the author of the novella, who, although he names neither the city nor the hotel, is of course clearly identifiable in its central character, standing outside his parents' house, his heart beating fearfully, anticipating the vision of his father's spirit as he heads north. Thomas Mann does not permit his Tonio Kröger to utter a single word of aesthetic disapproval about the two hotel lions. That he idealizes them, makes them appear harmless, even, has to do with the emboldening distance that comes with encountering them again, as if they had been transformed in his imagination.

In reality, what this fugacious son of Lübeck disliked about the city was its aesthetic bias: not only its indifference to his *Buddenbrooks* but also—or, indeed, on others' behalf—to the visual arts in general, and animal sculpture in particular. Had the city not shamefully overlooked another of its sons, the sculptor Fritz Behn, grandson of mayor Theodor Behn, for every conceivable project or commission? In the meantime, Behn, as Mann wrote in a letter to the editor of the *Lübecker Nachrichten* which appeared in the morning edition on 12 April 1913, had gone to Munich where he was now as professor at Royal Academy of Arts, and where, by the way, one could see what a real lion looked like—a *mighty porphyry lion* by none other than Behn himself, presiding over Munich's *grandest square*.

Fritz Behn was three years younger than Thomas Mann, and by the time *Tonio Kröger* was published, which was ten years before Mann's letter to the editor, it should already have been obvious to everyone that Lübeck lions could no longer be permitted to resemble those sleepy hotel sentinels. *To have discovered Fritz Behn, to have brought him into the light; Lübeck had its chance, but now it is too late.* This was the scorn that he vented from Munich over their mutual hometown—and as a prelude to which we may now see the ease with which Tonio Kröger passed the test and emancipated himself. Now he had found a fellow victim of the city's disregard, which allowed him to confront the readers of the *Lübecker Nachrichten* with the following sweeping generalization: *Lübeck appears incapable of believing that she might bring forth exceptional minds. Men whose nature and destiny will not allow them to follow the respectable Lübeckian path . . . What else? These men, who were a source of irritation and who were predicted to fail, are now out accomplishing things elsewhere, accomplishing a great many things. This will not do.*

This entire text, literally served up to the burghers with their breakfast, is dripping with implicit yet thoroughly unsubtle vitriol, at a time when, although Behn's porphyry lion may indeed have been stationed outside the Munich Secession, there was a new generation of artists in the process of 'seceding' from their teacher at the academy. And it is not as if the author of *Tonio Kröger* did not already have his fair share of prominent critics. As a 'champion' of the unfairly overlooked, he too was always a little too late. A typical Lübecker, you might say. And yet he had ended his 1913 article in the *Lübecker Nachrichten* on such a conciliatory note—as if already preparing for his 1926 lecture on the septuacentennial of the city's freedom, 'Lübeck as a spiritual form of life'. Had he not written in 1913: *Is one a Lübecker only if one trades in butter, wine or petroleum?* He discreetly neglected to mention grain, for what would the far-travelled artist be without his paternal inheritance? But the transition from complaints to hopes did imply that there must be 'recipients' for such things up there: *My accusations are my wishes. That Lübeck learn to believe in those who are her sons in unconventional ways.*

In other words, so much is clear in retrospect, Tonio Kröger had punished the hotel sentinels not by disdaining them but by rendering them harmless. These lions came from the wrong lion school, not from the capital of the Wittelsbachs but that of the Hohenzollerns. Just before the turn of the century, the Prussian lions had enjoyed a final high-point of their presence: on the National Memorial to Kaiser Wilhelm I by Reinhold Begas, menacingly perched on pedestals projecting over the steps, four lions kept watch over the allegorical spoils from the last war with France. For these lions, two additional sculptural specialists, Gaul and Kraus, had been commissioned, and the Berliners mockingly referred to the emperor both protected and trapped up there on his towering steed —whose reins only the spirit of Peace can hold—as 'Wilhelm in the lion's den'.

And yet half a century before, a Lübeck merchant, J. D. Jacobj, had commissioned two cast-iron lions from Christian Rauch's workshop, to be placed outside his house at 19 Große Petersgrube, where they would take up their posts in 1840. For the Free Imperial City, which had been dragged into two wars by Prussia, these exotic Berlin lions were probably more of a nuisance. Hence, what would seem bourgeois and conservative to Tonio Kröger—and it is true that in his old age, Rauch had tended to want to tame the grand gestures of neoclassicism —may at the time have struck the Lübeck bourgeoisie as more of an affront to patrician decency. In any case, the owner of Rauch's lions was never really allowed to enjoy this ostentatious display of taste and cultural refinement. The lions were sold and, in 1873, moved from the service of the bourgeoisie to that of the 'grand hotel', where it was not as important to be aware of what one could afford. Thus, when Tonio was still at the age of childish fears, they were already there, on either side of the hotel entrance. And they were still there on the night of Palm Sunday 1942, even when there was nothing left to guard or heraldically enhance.

When Thomas Mann returned to the city of his fathers in 1926 to give his celebratory speech on 'Lübeck as a spiritual form of life', it can only have been a small source of gratification to him that the city had approved the Reichsbank's application to establish a new building on the site of the old railway station on the condition that they furnish it with an important work of sculpture—and they had duly noted from whom the bank was to commission it. It would be another decade before anyone thought of a lion—in 1926, not even Thomas Mann would have recommended heraldic and heroic pathos. Instead, in a perfect demonstration of the workings of the zeitgeist, they opted for one of the lion's preferred species of prey: a gazelle by Fritz Behn. Some people might have preferred something by Ernst Barlach—but he would only find an advocate in Carl Georg Heise, who had set his sights on the niches in the oblique facade of St Catherine's church, until that project was cut short by the tyrannical enemies of degenerate art. The gazelle survived, even though it was made of bronze.

## Lions

First published as 'Verfehlte Illustration' (Misconceived Illustration) in 'Das Abwesende am Löwen. Glossen zum Bestiarium', *Neue Zürcher Zeitung* 153 (5–6 July 1986): 66.

*Avec plus de raison* . . . 'With better logic, we'd be winners in this fight / If my fellow lions could paint or draw'—*The Complete Fables of Jean de la Fontaine* (Norman B. Spector ed. and trans.) (Evanston: Northwestern University Press, 1988), p. 125; compare with 'Le lion abbatu par l'homme' in *Fables de La Fontaine: Illustrations par Grandville* (Paris: Garnier Frères, 1855), p. 120.

## Sympathy for the Lion

*It is curious* . . . See Alfred Polgar, 'Lotte bei den Löwen' [1929] in *Kleine Schriften*, VOL. 2, *Kreislauf* (Marcel Reich-Ranicki and Ulrich Weinzierl eds) (Reinbeck: Rowohlt, 1983), pp. 357–9.

## Homeopathy

*Similia similibus* 'Like cures like' (more precisely, *similia similibus curantur*), the foundational doctrine of homeopathy. The reference is to Christian Friedrich Hebbel, *Werke*, VOL. 5 (Gerhard Fricke, Werner Keller and Karl Pörnbacher eds) (Munich: Carl Hanser, 1967), p. 184. Misquoted (or paraphrased) by Hebbel from: Selig Cassel, 'Zum armen Heinrich Hartmanns von Aue' in *Weimarisches Jahrbuch für Deutsche Sprache, Literatur und Kunst*, VOL. 1 (Hoffmann von Fallersleben and Oskar Schade eds) (Hannover: Karl Rümpler, 1854), pp. 408–78; here, p. 412.

The original reference is to Vincent of Beauvais, *Speculum naturale* (lib. 20.74): 'Leo ex hominis visu febricitat. Denique febre semper quartana febricitat et tunc maxime carnes symiae appetit ut sanetur.' The concluding phrase, '*Similia similibus*', is Hebbel's own comment.

*Undoubtedly, Hebbel was a man-eater* . . . See Emil Kuh, *Biographie Friedrich Hebbels*, VOL. 2 (Vienna and Leipzig: Wilhelm Braumüller, 1912), pp. 487–8; Paul Bornstein, *Friedrich Hebbels Persönlichkeit. Gespräche, Urteile, Erinnerungen*, VOL. 2 (Berlin: Propyläen Verlag, 1924), p. 90–1. Emil Kuh (1828–76), Austrian writer and feuilletonist. Paul Bornstein (1868–1939), German writer and editor of the *Monatsschrift für neue Literatur und Kunst*.

*What for?* . . . Kuh, *Biographie*, p. 404; Bornstein, *Friedrich Hebbels Persönlichkeit*, VOL. 1 (Berlin: Propyläen Verlag, 1924), p. 318.

*He looked like a man* . . . See Bornstein, *Hebbels Persönlichkeit*, VOL. 2, p. 94. Karl Debrois van Bruyck (1828–1902), Austrian composer and music critic.

*Spare me that endless talk of the pleasures of nature* . . . Eduard Hanslick, *Aus meinem Leben*, VOL. 1 (Berlin: Allgemeiner Verein für Deutsche Literatur, 1894), p. 156. Eduard Hanslick (1825–1904), influential Austrian musicologist and critic.

*An absolute metaphor*: See Hans Blumenberg, *Paradigms for a Metaphorology* (Robert Savage trans.) (Ithaca, NY: Cornell University Press, 2010), p. 3.

## The Elephant, Not the Lion

*Disappointed with the lion* . . . See Arthur Schopenhauer, *Manuscript Remains*, VOL. 4, *The Manuscript Books of 1830–1852 and Last Manuscripts* (Arthur Hübscher ed. and E. F. J. Payne trans.) (Oxford: Berg, 1990), pp. 15–16:

> I expected that the *mating of the lion* as the extreme affirmation of the will in its most intense phenomenon would be accompanied by very vehement symptoms, and was surprised to find these were far below those that usually accompany the mating of humans. [Translation slightly modified.]

*The Idea of the elephant is imperishable* 'Die Idee des Elephanten ist unvergänglich'—I have been unable to find a direct source in Schopenhauer for this aphorism. It does occur, however, in Gustav Friedrich Wagner's *Encyklopädisches Register zu Schopenhauers Werken* (Karlsruhe: Braunsche, 1909), under the rubric 'Elephant'. Wagner lists two instances of the phrase, both in Chapter 41 in *The World as Will and Representation*, VOL. 2, yet the phrase does not occur in either location. Hence, I take it the aphorism is in fact a paraphrase by Wagner, and not a 'postulate' of Schopenhauer's at all. More puzzling still is the fact that in the same chapter, Schopenhauer comes very close to making the claim about the *lion*, not the elephant:

> [T]he lions that are born and that die are like the drops of the waterfall; but *leonitas*, the Idea or form or shape of the lion, is like the unshaken and unmoved rainbow on the waterfall.

—Arthur Schopenhauer, *The World as Will and Representation*, VOL. 2 (E. F. J. Payne trans.) (New York: Dover, 1966), p. 483.

*Disinterested delight* . . . See Immanuel Kant, *Critique of Aesthetic Judgement* (James Creed Meredith trans.) (Oxford: Clarendon Press, 1911), pp. 43–4 (§2).

'*Power to exist*' Arthur Schopenhauer, 'Fragments for the History of Philosophy' in *Parerga and Paralipomena*, VOL. 1 (E. F. J. Payne trans.) (Oxford: Clarendon Press, 1974), p. 87.

## The Absence About the Lion

A note on the title: 'Absence' is the defining characteristic of Blumenberg's lions. The word in German for absence is 'Abwesenheit' which, like the English, is derived from Latin *ab-esse*, 'to be away', 'not to be there'. Frequently, however, Blumenberg does not use 'Abwesenheit' to refer to this leonine absence but, rather, 'das Abwesende *am* Löwen', a nominalized adjective which is difficult to translate into English except by means of the rather inelegant 'the absent thing about the lion'. Unfortunately for the translator, this is a key term in Blumenberg's 'leonology'. Sometimes his lions are absent altogether, but more often they are deficient, lacking or marked by absence in some

way, either literally or figuratively. In the case of this particular 'lion', the title might be translated as 'what the lion
was missing' (i.e. one of his eyes), but as this phrase recurs
in several other guises throughout the text, it seemed advis-
able to retain the word 'absence'. In order to preserve the
distinction between 'die Abwesenheit *des* Löwen' and 'das
Abwesende *am* Löwen', however, I have translated the
former as 'the absence *of*' and the latter as 'the absence
*about* the lion'.

*They roared so dreadfully* . . . Anna Grigoryevna Dostoyevskaya,
   *The Diary of Dostoyevski's Wife* (René Fülöp-Miller
   and Friedrich Eckstein eds, and Madge Pemberton trans.)
   (London: Gollancz, 1928), p. 123.

## Fiesco's Lion

*Tell me not of that lion* . . . This and all subsequent quotations are
   from Friedrich Schiller, 'Fiesco: Or, the Genoese Conspiracy'
   (Henry G. Bohn trans.) in *The Works of Frederick Schiller*,
   VOL. 4, *Early Dramas and Romances* (London: Bell and Daldy,
   1867), pp. 165–8. [Translation partially modified.]

## Impeded Lions

*The Sleeping Gypsy* Henri Rousseau, *La Bohémienne endormie*
   (1897), oil on canvas, Museum of Modern Art, New York,
   USA.

*The Hungry Lion* Henri Rousseau, *Le Lion, ayant faim, se jette
   sur l'antilope* (1905), oil on canvas, Fondation Beyeler,
   Riehen, Switzerland.

### One Species of Leonine Absence

*But for human beings, that is already a lot* Odo Marquard, 'Unburdenings: Theodicy Motives in Modern Philosophy' in *In Defense of the Accidental: Philosophical Studies* (Robert M. Wallace trans.) (Oxford: Oxford University Press, 1991), pp. 8–28; here, p. 25.

*Philosophy is too hard for human beings* Carl Friedrich von Weizsäcker, 'Die Wissenschaft ist noch nicht erwachsen', *Die Zeit* (10 October 1980). Weizsäcker (1912–2007), German physicist and philosopher, who worked with Werner Heisenberg and others during Second World War on the development of the nuclear bomb in Germany.

*Cur aliquid potius quam nihil* 'Why is there something rather than nothing?' See Gottfried Wilhelm Leibniz, 'On the Ultimate Origination of Things' in *Philosophical Essays* (Roger Ariew and Daniel Garber eds and trans) (Indianapolis: Hackett, 1989), pp. 149–54; here, p. 150.

*Causa sui ipsius* 'his own cause', self-originating; see Hans Blumenberg, *Ein mögliches Selbstverständnis* (Stuttgart: Reclam, 1997), pp. 71–4.

*Cur potius leo quam nequaquam* 'Why is there a lion rather than none at all?'

### Ecclesiastes' Dead Lion

*Qōheleth* [תֶלָהֹק] the Hebrew title of the book of Ecclesiastes.

*Melior est canis vivens leone mortuo* . . . Ecclesiastes 9:4.

*Heretical undercurrent* . . . See 'The Acts of the Holy Apostle Thomas' in *New Testament Apocrypha*, VOL. 2, *Writings*

*Relating to the Apostles, Apocalypses and Related Subjects*
(Edgar Hennecke revd., Wilhelm Schneemelcher ed. and
Robert McLachlan Wilson trans.) (Louisville, KY: West-
minster John Knox Press, 2003), pp. 339–411; here, p. 352.

*Et laudavi magis mortuous quam viventes . . .* 'Wherefore I
praised the dead which are already dead more than the
living which are yet alive. Yea, better is he than both they,
which hath not yet been, who hath not seen the evil work
that is done under the sun' (Ecclesiastes 4:2–3).

*Johnson immediately knew . . .* See James Boswell, *The Life of
Samuel Johnson*, VOL. 2 (London, 1791), p. 191. All subsequent references are to this page.

*In the preface to his novel . . .* Eduard von Keyserling, *Fräulein
Rosa Herz. Eine Kleinstadtliebe* (Dresden: Verlag Heinrich
Minden, 1887).

*Rosalie, the ballet master's daughter . . .* This refers to Rosa,
the protagonist of the Keyserling's novel.

## The Absence About the Lion: Morgenstern

*A leaf of a calendar . . .* Christian Morgenstern, 'The Lion' in
*The Gallows Songs: Christian Morgenstern's Galgenlieder.
A Selection* (Max Knight introd. and trans.) (Berkeley:
University of California Press, 1966), p. 91.

*Leo rugiens quaerens quem devoret* 'Be sober, be vigilant;
because your adversary the devil, as a roaring lion, walketh
about, seeking whom he may devour' (1 Peter 5:8).

### The Absent Lion

Originally published in *Gerade noch Klassiker. Glossen zu Fontane* (Munich: Hanser, 1998), p. 144.

*I find it really first rate . . .* Theodor Fontane, 'Letter to Georg Friedlaender, 4 July 1893' in *Werke, Schriften und Briefe, Part 4: Briefe* VOL. 4 (Otto Drude, Helmuth Nürnberger and Christian Andree eds) (Munich: Hanser, 1982), pp. 264–65.

*Triumph of the species* 'Triumph der Gattung', which could also mean 'triumph of the genre'.

### Preserved from a Lion

Originally published in *Gerade noch Klassiker. Glossen zu Fontane* (Munich: Hanser, 1998), pp. 149–52.

*Samlede verker* In Norwegian in the original; literally, 'collected works'.

*'Ninny' and 'chatterbox'* 'Schafslise' and 'Quatschliese'; roughly, 'sheep-Lisa' and 'prattle-Lizzie' respectively. These pejoratives appear to be Fontane's own coinage. The first appears in a letter to Friedrich Spielhagen (16 February 1897): 'I turn away in disgust from these forms of love and for their practitioners (Nora tops the list) I have only the name: *Schafslise*.' The second is used in a letter to Friedrich Stephany (22 March 1898): 'the much-admired Nora is the greatest *Quatschliese* ever to have spoken down to an audience from the stage'—Fontane, *Briefe*, VOL. 4, pp. 636 and 704.

*Ibsen's truth* Letter to Stephany (22 March 1898), ibid.

*In the end he was . . . an apothecary* Letter to Stephany (17 May 1898), ibid., p. 720.

*Days of sittings, days of painting* See Fontane's letter to his daughter Mete (19 March 1896), ibid., p. 544.

### The Baptized Lion

*To the beasts with the man!* Quoted from 'The Acts of Paul', *New Testament Apocrypha*, VOL. 2, pp. 213–70; here, p. 251.

*Come let us see the man . . .* Ibid., p. 253.

*Out of the valley of the burying ground* Ibid., p. 264.

*But it did not touch Paul or the lion* Ibid., p. 253.

*A man small of stature* Ibid., p. 239.

### The Renewed Absence of Leonine Thought

*Regal lethargy . . .* An oblique reference to Schopenhauer. See note on 'The Elephant, Not the Lion' in this volume.

*And so he invented the prototypical concept: the trap. . .* See Hans Blumenberg, *Theorie der Unbegrifflichkeit* (Anselm Haverkamp ed.) (Frankfurt: Suhrkamp, 2007), p. 10.

### Two Different Measures of a Lion's Hunger

*When Deussen visited Nietzsche . . .* The visit is recounted in *Conversations with Nietzsche: A Life in the Words of His Contemporaries* (Sander L. Gilman ed. and David J. Parent trans.) (New York and Oxford: Oxford University Press, 1987), p. 200. See also Meta von Salis-Marschlins, *Philosoph und Edelmensch. Ein Beitrag zur Charakteristik Friedrich Nietzsches* (Leipzig: C. F. Naumann, 1897), p. 47.

*Pensiveness* In German 'Nachdenklichkeit'. See Hans Blumenberg, 'Pensiveness' (David Adams trans.), *Caliban* 6 (1989): 51–5.

*Strip off the theological bearskin* . . . From Friedrich Nietzsche's letter to Paul Deussen (Autumn 1866). See Paul Deussen, *Erinnerungen an Friedrich Nietzsche* (Leipzig: Brockhaus, 1901), pp. 27–29; see also *Conversations with Nietzsche*, p. 25.

## The Cares of the Lioness

*The gaze, grown weary* . . . See Rainer Maria Rilke, 'The Panther' in *New Poems* (Edward Snow trans.) (San Francisco: North Point Press, 1984), p. 73.

*Reoccupation* In German 'Umbesetzung'—an important term in Blumenberg's *Legitimität der Neuzeit* (1966). I follow Robert Wallace's lead here in rendering it as 'reoccupation', although this translation obscures the theatrical resonance of the word. An alternative translation might be 'recasting'. For a more comprehensive analysis, see Hans Blumenberg, *The Legitimacy of the Modern Age* (Robert M. Wallace trans.) (Cambridge, MA: MIT Press, 1985), pp. *xx–xxv*; and *The Laughter of the Thracian Woman: A Protohistory of Theory* (Spencer Hawkins trans.) (New York: Bloomsbury Academic, 2015), pp. 29–45.

*Being sick doesn't concern him* Rainer Maria Rilke, 'The Lion Cage' in *Ahead of All Parting: The Selected Poetry and Prose of Rainer Maria Rilke* (Stephen Mitchell ed. and trans.) (New York: Modern Library, 1995), pp. 281–2; here, p. 281.

### The Fearful Lion

*Nobody wanted to appear old-fashioned* . . . Marta Feuchtwanger, *Nur eine Frau: Jahre, Tage, Stunden* (Munich and Vienna: Langen Müller, 1984), p. 131.

*Someone else had shot the lion* . . . Ibid.; see also Marta Feuchtwanger, *An Émigré Life: Munich, Berlin, Sanary, Pacific Palisades*, interviewed by Lawrence M. Weschler, VOL. 1 (Los Angeles: University of California, 1976), pp. 319–20. The critic in question is Alfred Mayer (1860–1932), who, in 1917, at the age of fifty-seven, married Elisabeth Holnstein who was twenty-four—she is better known as translator and publisher Noa Kiepenheuer (1893–1971). According to Feuchtwanger, the joke about the man and the lion stems from the artist, writer and collector Rolf von Hoerschelmann (1885–1947).

### The Dreamt-Out Dream of the Lion's Absence

*Such a darling little war* Alfred Polgar, 'Romain Rolland: Die Zeit wird kommen' in *Kleine Schriften*, VOL. 5 (Marcel Reich-Ranicki and Ulrich Weinzierl eds) (Reinbeck: Rowohlt, 1985), pp. 207–9

*Are Prophets Good for Anything?* Alfred Polgar, 'Nützen die Propheten? (Über Romain Rolland)' in *Kleine Schriften*, VOL. 4 (Marcel Reich-Ranicki and Ulrich Weinzierl eds) (Reinbeck: Rowohlt, 1984), pp. 34–5.

*Advocatus agni* literally, 'lamb's advocate', see Polgar, 'Fritz von Unruh: Heinrich aus Andernach' in *Kleine Schriften*, VOL. 5, pp. 396–8; here, p. 397.

*Either the lion will have lost his claws* Polgar, 'Julius Hay: Das Neue Paradies' in *Kleine Schriften*, VOL. 5, pp. 549–52; here, p. 549.

### In Defence of the Absent Lion

Originally published (without the last three paragraphs) as 'Die Rettung des Fabellöwen durch Wittgenstein', *Neue Zürcher Zeitung* 242 (17–18 October 1992), p. 67.

*Explicit 'retraction'* See Ludwig Wittgenstein, *Remarks on the Foundations of Mathematics* (G. H. von Wright, R. Rhees and G. E. M. Anscombe eds, and G. E. M. Anscombe trans.) (Cambridge, MA: MIT Press, 1967), pp. 181–3. Unless otherwise noted, all further quotations refer to these three pages.

*Distillations of significance* See Hans Blumenberg, *Work on Myth* (Robert M. Wallace trans.) (Cambridge, MA: MIT Press, 1985), pp. 59–112.

*Until further notice*! In German 'Bis auf weiteres!', which also means 'for the time being!' See Hans Blumenberg, *Die verführbahrkeit des Philosophen* (Berlin: Suhrkamp, 2000), p. 165: 'So philosophieren wir, wenn's zu sagen erlaubt ist, *bis auf weiteres.*' Anselm Haverkamp uses this phrase as an epigraph to his essay, 'The Scandal of Metaphorology' (Barbara Natalie Nagel and Daniel Hoffman-Schwartz trans), *Telos* 158 (Spring 2012): 37–58.

*Of course I want to be perfect* This exchange is reported in *Ludwig Wittgenstein: Personal Recollections* (Rush Rhees ed.) (Oxford: Basil Blackwell, 1981), p. 50.

*A hint from the gods* . . . Wittgenstein, *Remarks*, p. 130.

### Delayed Effects of Absent Lions

*Patience Rewarded* 'Zur Eröffnung des Zoologischen Gartens Zürich. Die belohnte Geduld', *Neue Zürcher Zeitung* (8 September 1929) Section D: 1.

### The Absence About the Sea Lion

*Atlantic coast* See Heinz Guderian, *Panzer Leader* (Constantine Fitzgibbon trans.) (London: Penguin, 2000), p. 113.

*As a last resort . . .* See *Hitler: Speeches and Proclamations 1932–1945. The Chronicle of a Dictatorship*, VOL. 3, *1939–1940* (Max Domarus ed. and Chris Wilcox trans.) (Wauconda, IL: Bolchazy-Carducci, 1997), p. 2039.

*First-class oceanic naval power* See Gerhard Schreiber, Bernd Stegemann and Detlef Vogel (eds), *Germany and the Second World War*, VOL. 3, *The Mediterranean, South-East Europe, and North Africa 1939–1941* (Dean S. McMurry, Ewald Osers and Louise Willmot trans) (Oxford: Clarendon Press, 1995), pp. 292–3.

### The Polemical Lion

*Schopenhauer's disappointment* See note on 'The Elephant, Not the Lion' in this volume.

*Hena alla leonta* ["Ενα ἀλλὰ λέοντα] Literally, 'one but a lion'. Aesop, 'La Lionne et le renard / Λέαινα καὶ ἀλώπηξ' in *Fables* (Émile Chambry ed. and trans.) (Paris: Les Belles Lettres, 1927), p. 84. See also Hans Blumenberg, 'Glossen zu Fabeln', *Akzente* 28(4) (1981): 340–4; here, p. 342.

*To vent his . . . spleen on August von Platen* Refers to German poet and dramatist, August Graf von Platen-Hallermünde

(1796–1835). On Heine's bitter public feud with Platen, the so-called Platen-Affäre, see Karl Kraus, 'Heine and the Consequences' in *The Kraus Project* (Jonathan Franzen ed. and trans.) (New York: Farrar, Straus and Giroux, 2013), pp. 3–133.

*The lioness does not first bring forth a rabbit* This and the following two quotations are from Heinrich Heine, 'The Baths of Lucca' in *Pictures of Travel* (Charles Godfrey Leland trans.) (Philadelphia: Schaefer and Koradi, 1879), pp. 302–65; here, p. 358. [Translation modified.]

*Everything is of importance to science* Ibid., p. 361.

### The Presence of a Lion—As If He Were Absent

*Thus the three creatures did no harm to one another* See *The Midrash on Psalms* (*Midrash Tehillim*), VOL. 2 (William G. Braude trans.) (New Haven: Yale University Press, 1959), pp. 175, 505n26. The 'yellow wolf' may in fact be a jackal.

### The Remedy for the Return of the Lion

*Laughed as in days of good health* See Hans Carossa, *Der Tag des jungen Arztes* (Wiesbaden: Insel Verlag, 1955), p. 221.

### Sea Lions—A Misunderstanding

*Unusual publicity stunt* The incident was reported in the *Frankfurter Allgemeine Zeitung* (13 May 1987) which is where Blumenberg read about it.

### The Absence About the Lion: St Jerome in His Study with an Hourglass

This was also published in Hans Blumenberg, *Der Mann vom Mond—Über Ernst Jünger* (Alexander Schmitz and Marcel Lepper eds) (Frankfurt: Suhrkamp, 2007), pp. 126–7.

*The roaring lion of the Psalms* In fact, the reference is to the First Epistle of Peter (see 1 Peter 5:8).

*To the gate of timeless gardens, where no hour tolls* Ernst Jünger, 'Das Sanduhrbuch' [1954] in *Sämtliche Werke*, VOL. 12 (Stuttgart: Klett-Cotta, 1979), pp. 101–249; here, p. 230.

*Who wouldn't want to partake of this stillness* Ibid., p. 104.

### Conciliatory Expulsion of the Lion

*O you weak king!* See Samuel A. Berman, *Midrash Tanhuma–Yelammedenu: An English Translation of Genesis and Exodus from the Printed Version of Tanhuma-Yelammedenu with an Introduction, Notes, and Indexes* (Hoboken: KTAV Publishing House, 1996), p. 266. [Translation modified.]

*The lion, which is the mightiest among beasts* Proverbs 30:30.

### The Liberating Power of the Truth

*Meliora omnium philosophorum* 'better than all philosophers.' See Martin Luther, '3490: Aesopi commendatio' in *Werke. Kritische Gesamtausgabe, Part 2: Tischreden*, VOL. 3, *Tischreden aus den dreißiger Jahren* (Weimar: Böhlau, 1914), pp. 353–5; here, p. 353.

*Non ubique omnia esse dicenda* 'not everything must be said everywhere', ibid.

*Non licet quaecunque dicere* 'one is not permitted to say just anything', ibid., p. 354.

### The False Lion of the Bacchae

*Kabod* [דּוֹבָּכ] 'glory'; see Exodus 33:18–20.

*Alien god* See Hans Jonas, *The Gnostic Religion: The Message of the Alien God and the Beginnings of Christianity*, 3rd EDN (Boston: Beacon Press, 2001).

*Taurokerōn theon* [ταυρόκερων θεὸν] 'Bull-horned god'; see Euripides, 'Bacchae' in *The Tragedies of Euripides* (T. A. Buckley trans.) (London: Henry G. Bohn, 1850), v. 100.

*Hieron endyton* [ἱερὸν ἐνδυτόν] Ibid., v. 137.

*Hunting the blood of the slain goat* . . . Ibid, vv. 137–8.

*Already the bull* Ibid., vv. 920–22: 'And you seem to lead me, being like a bull and horns seem to grow on your head. But were you ever before a beast? For you have certainly now become a bull [τεταύρωσαι γὰρ οὖν].'

*Hēssōn oudenos theōn* [ἥσσων οὐδενὸς θεῶν] 'Inferior to none of the gods', ibid., v. 777.

*That most polysemous of mythical attributes 'deinos'* [δεινός] means both 'terrible' and 'wonderful'. See Sophocles' *Antigone*, vv. 332–3: πολλὰ τὰ δεινὰ κοὐδὲν ἀνθρώπου δεινότερον πέλει [Many are the things of terror (or wonder) but nothing is more terrible (or wonderful) than man]. On the inherent ambiguity of the term, see Martin Heidegger, *Introduction to Metaphysics* (Gregory Fried and Richard

Polt trans) (New Haven: Yale University Press, 2000), pp. 156–76.

*Dionysus' vision* Euripides, 'Bacchae', vv. 971–6.

*His mother, as priestess, began the slaughter* . . . Ibid., vv. 1114–15.

*Atē* ['Aτη] The Greek goddess of delusion, blind folly and ruin.

*He was not born from a woman's blood* . . . Euripides, 'Bacchae', vv. 989–91.

*Yes, for I suffered terrible things* . . . Ibid., vv. 1377–8.

*Pollai morphai tōn daimoniōn* [πολλαὶ μορφαὶ τῶν δαιμονίων] 'Many are the forms of divine things, and the gods bring to pass many things unexpectedly', ibid., vv. 1388–9.

*You have learnt it too late* . . . Ibid., v. 1345.

*Only a god may prevail against a god* 'Nemo contra deum nisi deus ipse'; see Johann Wolfgang von Goethe, *Collected Works*, VOL. 5, *From My Life: Poetry and Truth, Part 4* (Thomas P. Saine and Jeffrey L. Sammons eds, and Robert R. Heitner trans.) (Princeton, NJ: Princeton University Press, 1987), p. 598. For Blumenberg's extensive discussion of this 'extraordinary saying', see *Work on Myth*, pp. 523–56.

### Felicitous Animal Metaphor

Lothar Späth (1937–2016), German politician (CDU), minister-president of Baden-Württemberg from 1978 to 1991.

Oskar Lafontaine (b. 1943), German politician, member of Social Democratic Party (SPD), minister-president of

Saarland from 1985 to 1998. At the time, Lafontaine was deputy chairman of the SPD.

*In the den of the lionesses* See Eckhard Fuhr, 'Ein gemütliches Streitgespräch zweier politischer Hoffnungsträger' [A Convivial Debate between Two Political Hopefuls], *Frankfurter Allgemeine Zeitung* (6 March 1989).

*Platzhirsch* literally, the dominant, alpha male on the rutting ground ('Brunftplatz'); in its metaphorical sense, roughly equivalent to the English 'top dog'.

*Clearing of Being* . . . See Martin Heidegger, 'Letter on Humanism' (Frank A. Capuzzi trans. with J. Glenn Gray) in *Basic Writings* (David Farrell Krell ed.) (London: Harper Perennial, 2008), pp. 213–65; here, p. 230.

## Tonio Kröger's Lions

*There was the hotel* . . . Thomas Mann, 'Tonio Kröger' in *Death in Venice and Other Tales* (Joachim Neugroschel trans.) (London: Penguin, 1998), pp. 161–228; here, p. 199. [Translation slightly modified.] All other quotations from this story are from pp. 196–208.

*Palm Sunday 1942* Blumenberg's parents' house was also destroyed in the Allied bombing of Lübeck on 29 March 1942.

*Mighty porphyry lion* Thomas Mann, 'Für Fritz Behn' in *Große kommentierte Frankfurter Ausgabe. Werke–Briefe–Tagebücher*, VOL. 14.1, *Essays I (1893–1914)* (Heinrich Detering and Stephan Stachorski eds) (Frankfurt: S. Fischer, 2002), pp. 363–71; here, p. 366.